NEW STANDARD REVISED EDITION

the

CURTIS CREEK MANIFESTO

BEING A BASIC GUIDE TO THE ART of FLY FISHING ON MOVING WATER...

WRITTEN, CONCEIVED, AND ILLUSTRATED BY SHERIDAN ANDERSON

PREAMBLE AND OPENING SALVOS

THE MAJOR DIFFICULTY WITH MOST HOW-TO FISHING BOOKS IS THAT OF TRYING TO FIGURE OUT WHAT THE AUTHOR IS TALKING ABOUT - THE BEGINNER IS ASSAULTED WITH PAGE AFTER PAGE OF TEXT WHICH HE MUST TRANSLATE INTO VISUAL IMAGES BEFORE HE CAN EVEN BEGIN TO UNDERSTAND IT. ALSO, MOST PRIMERS FAIL BECAUSE THEY ARE SO HIGHLY OVERWRITTEN THAT THE NOVICE BECOMES HOPELESSLY BURIED UNDER AN AVALANCHE OF INFORMATION, MUCH OF WHICH IS ONLY VAGUELY INCIDENTAL TO A FIRM GRASP OF THE BASICS AND THUS SERVING ONLY TO CONFUSE THE ISSUE... IN ACTUALITY, MOST ANGLERS LEARN HOW TO FISH IN SPITE OF THE TEXTBOOKS, RATHER THAN BECAUSE OF THEM.

HERE THEN IS THE CURTIS CREEK MANIFESTO, A UNIQUE AND VERY VISUAL WORK DESIGNED TO ELIMINATE THE GUESSWORK AND CONFUSION INHERENT IN ORTHODOX TEXTBOOKS WHICH RELY TOO HEAVILY ON THE PRINTED WORD. THIS HIGHLY GRAPHIC PRIMER IS A DISTILLATION OF ALMOST NINTY YEARS OF FLY FISHING EXPERIENCE (THIRTY YEARS OF MY OWN/ SIXTY YEARS OF MY MENTOR, UNCLE AND COLLABORATOR, GRANT WOOTTON.) THE MANIFESTO WON'T GUARANTEE A POSY OF TROUT ON YOUR NEXT FISHING TRIP BUT IT WILL SET YOU SOLIDLY ON THE RIGHT PATH TO BECOMING A WORTHY ANGLER.

READ IT THROUGH AT LEAST TWICE AND TAKE IT ALONG WHEN YOU GO FISHING TO USE AS A REFERENCE. IF POSSIBLE, LATCH ONTO A KNOWLEDGEABLE ANGLER TO GO FISHING WITH - A GOOD TEACHER IS WORTH MORE THAN ALL THE ANGLING LITERATURE EVER WRITTEN ... DON'T FORGET TO SEND HIM A CARD ON HIS BIRTHDAY AND A BOTTLE OF FANCY BOOZE AT CHRISTMAS TIME.

THE ELEVEN COMMANDMENTS

Thou shalt know thy knots well and rig thy gear in an artful manner.

Thou shalt cast with precision and thy fly shalt like a cobweb alight.

Thou shalt fish upstream.

Thou shalt know thy waters and be wise about those things upon which thy prey doth feed.

Thou shalt cunningly plan thy strategy in advance of each hole, pocket and riffle.

Let not thy shadow nor that of thy rod fall upon the waters.

Thou shalt move with stealth and keep thyself low and in deepest shadow and ever secret thyself behind tree, rock, hummock and shrub.

Thou shalt keep thy rod behind thee and thy line in readiness until thou art ready to cast.

Thou shalt avoid fly-drag like the plague and watch thy lure like a hawk.

Thou shalt strike quickly but gently and thou shalt hopefully release thy quarry to fight another day.

Thou shalt love the waters and all things that nourish therefrom; and thou shalt cherish and protect them as thine own ~ For all nature is thy home and all living things are thy kin.

SHERIDAN ANDERSON

THIS SIMPLE IMPERATIVE IS THE KEY TO CATCHING FISH:

MUSN'T SCARE!

- GOLDEN
- CUTTHROAT
- WHITEFISH
- LAKE TROUT

HEAVY DUTY FISH FRIGHTENERS:

VIBRATIONS

CARNIVORES — IF YOU CAN SEE THE FISH, THEY CAN SEE YOU.

SHADOWS

RAPID WATER-LEVEL CHANGES

STRANGE MOVEMENT — EVEN YOUR ROD TIP

SUDDEN RAIN

OTHER SCARED FISH

A SLOPPY CAST

LUNKERS

INDISCREET PICK-UP

— ETC. AND SO FORTH...

YOU CAN'T AVOID SCARING SOME OF THE FISH, BUT THE LESS YOU SCARE, THE MORE YOU CATCH...

- BROWN TROUT
- BROOKIE
- RAINBOW
- GRAYLING

ON THE NEXT PAGE I REVEAL SOME OF THE MASTERFUL STRATEGY THAT ENABLED ME TO KEEP A TOWN OF 11,000 ALIVE UNTIL AN AIR-DROP COULD BE IMPLEMENTED...

FISH UPSTREAM 👉

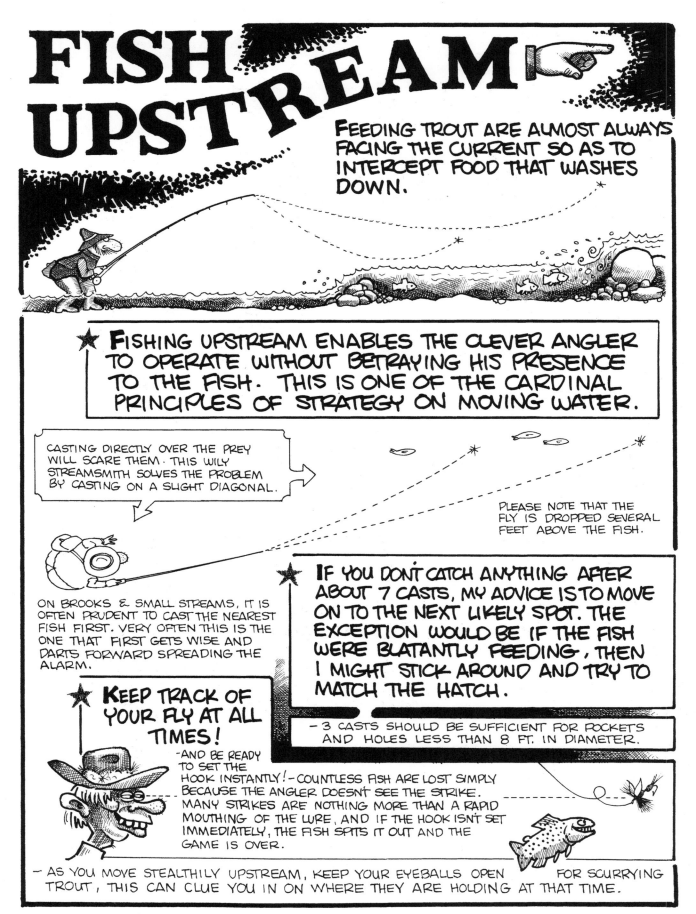

FEEDING TROUT ARE ALMOST ALWAYS FACING THE CURRENT SO AS TO INTERCEPT FOOD THAT WASHES DOWN.

★ FISHING UPSTREAM ENABLES THE CLEVER ANGLER TO OPERATE WITHOUT BETRAYING HIS PRESENCE TO THE FISH. THIS IS ONE OF THE CARDINAL PRINCIPLES OF STRATEGY ON MOVING WATER.

CASTING DIRECTLY OVER THE PREY WILL SCARE THEM. THIS WILY STREAMSMITH SOLVES THE PROBLEM BY CASTING ON A SLIGHT DIAGONAL.

PLEASE NOTE THAT THE FLY IS DROPPED SEVERAL FEET ABOVE THE FISH.

ON BROOKS & SMALL STREAMS, IT IS OFTEN PRUDENT TO CAST THE NEAREST FISH FIRST. VERY OFTEN THIS IS THE ONE THAT FIRST GETS WISE AND DARTS FORWARD SPREADING THE ALARM.

★ IF YOU DON'T CATCH ANYTHING AFTER ABOUT 7 CASTS, MY ADVICE IS TO MOVE ON TO THE NEXT LIKELY SPOT. THE EXCEPTION WOULD BE IF THE FISH WERE BLATANTLY FEEDING, THEN I MIGHT STICK AROUND AND TRY TO MATCH THE HATCH.

- 3 CASTS SHOULD BE SUFFICIENT FOR POCKETS AND HOLES LESS THAN 8 FT. IN DIAMETER.

★ KEEP TRACK OF YOUR FLY AT ALL TIMES!

- AND BE READY TO SET THE HOOK INSTANTLY! - COUNTLESS FISH ARE LOST SIMPLY BECAUSE THE ANGLER DOESN'T SEE THE STRIKE. MANY STRIKES ARE NOTHING MORE THAN A RAPID MOUTHING OF THE LURE, AND IF THE HOOK ISN'T SET IMMEDIATELY, THE FISH SPITS IT OUT AND THE GAME IS OVER.

- AS YOU MOVE STEALTHILY UPSTREAM, KEEP YOUR EYEBALLS OPEN FOR SCURRYING TROUT, THIS CAN CLUE YOU IN ON WHERE THEY ARE HOLDING AT THAT TIME.

REFRACTION

WITHOUT BURDENING YOU WITH THE DREARY TECHNICALITIES, SUFFICE IT TO SAY THAT THE WATER BENDS THE LIGHT RAYS IN SUCH A MANNER THAT THE ANGLER APPEARS CLOSER TO THE FISH THAN HE ACTUALLY IS. IN FACT, UNDER CERTAIN CONDITIONS THE TROUT CAN SEE US EVEN WHEN WE ARE BEYOND THEIR LINE OF HORIZON.

WITH THIS IN MIND YOU CAN SEE WHY IT IS NECESSARY TO STAY VERY LOW WHEN APPROACHING YOUR QUARRY — EVEN WHEN FISHING UPSTREAM —

— **B**UT ESPECIALLY WHEN APPROACHING FROM THE SIDE...

THE RULE IS: THE CLOSER — THE LOWER. WHERE COVER IS SPARSE YOU MIGHT WELL KEEP BACK 30 FEET FROM THE BANK AND DO ALL YOUR CASTING FROM A KNEELING POSITION. KEEP YOUR ROD LOW AND BEHIND YOU UNTIL YOU'RE READY TO CAST...

ON THE FOLLOWING PAGE I UNVEIL THE PEERLESS TECHNIQUES THAT I EMPLOYED IN ORDER TO CATCH ENOUGH FISH TO PREVENT THE RAGING FLOODWATERS FROM TOPPING THE LEVEES AT LIZARD BEND MONTANA. THUS WITH THE AID OF ARCHIMEDE'S PRINCIPLE DID I AVERT IMMINENT DISASTER TO THE ENTIRE MISSOURI BASIN...

STALKING

–THE SNEAKY ART OF APPROACH

THE FLY CAN BE ATTACHED TO THE KEEPER RING OR LEFT TRAILING IN THE WATER. IF POSSIBLE, REEL-OUT THE CORRECT AMOUNT OF LINE SO YOU WON'T NEED MORE THAN ONE FALSE-CAST.

THE UPSTREAM CRAWL

–ORIGINATED BY THE MARQUIS DE SADE IN FEBRUARY OF 1764...

THE ART OF STALKING IS ALMOST UNKNOWN IN THE U.S.A., YET IT IS THE MOST EFFECTIVE TACTIC IN FLY FISHING. PERHAPS THIS OVERSIGHT IS DUE TO SOME VAGUE PURITANICAL CONCEPT THAT EQUATES KNEELING, STOOPING, AND CRAWLING WITH SELF-ABASEMENT UNLESS CONFINED TO THE PEW. THE MEDIA HAS ALSO UNWITTINGLY REINFORCED THIS CONDITIONING — I DON'T RECALL EVER SEEING THE COVER OF A FISHING GAZETTE DEPICTING AN ANGLER ON HIS KNEES, MUCH LESS CRAWLING.

STAY LOW AND TRY AND KEEP A BUSH, TREE, OR ROCK BETWEEN YOU AND THE FISH.

NO QUICK MOVEMENTS! ADVANCE SLOWLY TO THE SPOT FROM WHICH YOU INTEND TO CAST.

IF POSSIBLE, STAY IN THE SHADOWS & DON'T BRANDISH THAT ROD UNTIL READY TO CAST.

THE BEGINNER WILL LEARN STALKING BEST BY FISHING FROM SHORE WHENEVER POSSIBLE. NOVICE ANGLERS RELY TOO HEAVILY ON WADERS AND HIP-BOOTS.

AN EXPERT SNEAK WILL EXERT CONSIDERABLE PHYSICAL AND MENTAL ENERGY TO THE ART. HE WILL TAKE TIME TO PLAN THE APPROACH TO EACH HOLDING STATION — TO HIM, THE WATER BECOMES A GLORIOUS, SHIMMERING THREE-DIMENSIONAL CHESSBOARD, A GAME TO BE MASTERED THRU SKILL, DILIGENCE, AND IMAGINATION.

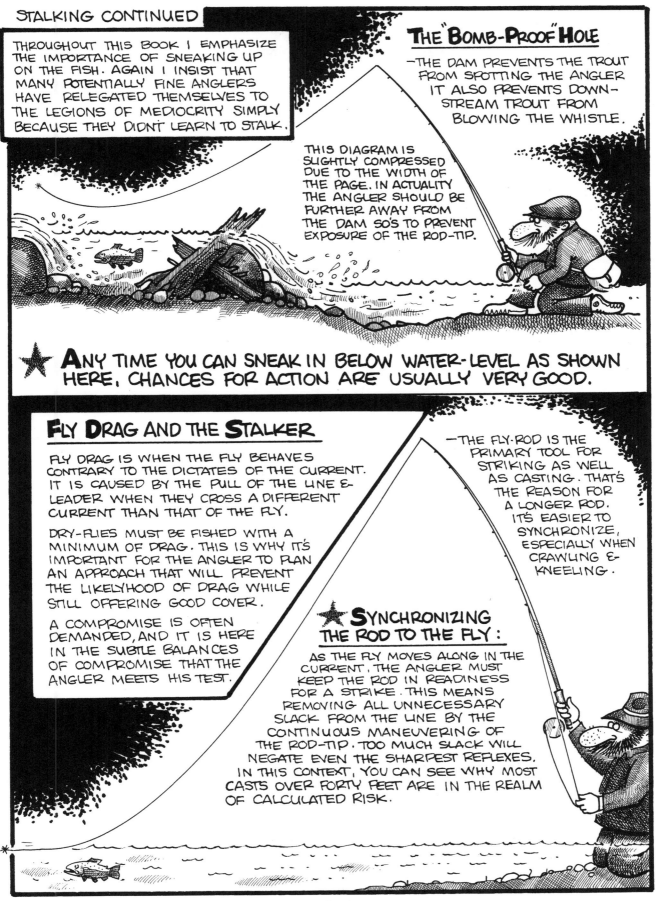

THROUGHOUT THIS BOOK I EMPHASIZE THE IMPORTANCE OF SNEAKING UP ON THE FISH. AGAIN I INSIST THAT MANY POTENTIALLY FINE ANGLERS HAVE RELEGATED THEMSELVES TO THE LEGIONS OF MEDIOCRITY SIMPLY BECAUSE THEY DIDN'T LEARN TO STALK.

THE "BOMB-PROOF" HOLE

—THE DAM PREVENTS THE TROUT FROM SPOTTING THE ANGLER. IT ALSO PREVENTS DOWN-STREAM TROUT FROM BLOWING THE WHISTLE.

THIS DIAGRAM IS SLIGHTLY COMPRESSED DUE TO THE WIDTH OF THE PAGE. IN ACTUALITY THE ANGLER SHOULD BE FURTHER AWAY FROM THE DAM SO'S TO PREVENT EXPOSURE OF THE ROD-TIP.

★ ANY TIME YOU CAN SNEAK IN BELOW WATER-LEVEL AS SHOWN HERE, CHANCES FOR ACTION ARE USUALLY VERY GOOD.

FLY DRAG AND THE STALKER

FLY DRAG IS WHEN THE FLY BEHAVES CONTRARY TO THE DICTATES OF THE CURRENT. IT IS CAUSED BY THE PULL OF THE LINE & LEADER WHEN THEY CROSS A DIFFERENT CURRENT THAN THAT OF THE FLY.

DRY-FLIES MUST BE FISHED WITH A MINIMUM OF DRAG. THIS IS WHY IT'S IMPORTANT FOR THE ANGLER TO PLAN AN APPROACH THAT WILL PREVENT THE LIKELYHOOD OF DRAG WHILE STILL OFFERING GOOD COVER.

A COMPROMISE IS OFTEN DEMANDED, AND IT IS HERE IN THE SUBTLE BALANCES OF COMPROMISE THAT THE ANGLER MEETS HIS TEST.

—THE FLY-ROD IS THE PRIMARY TOOL FOR STRIKING AS WELL AS CASTING. THAT'S THE REASON FOR A LONGER ROD. IT'S EASIER TO SYNCHRONIZE, ESPECIALLY WHEN CRAWLING & KNEELING.

★ SYNCHRONIZING THE ROD TO THE FLY:

AS THE FLY MOVES ALONG IN THE CURRENT, THE ANGLER MUST KEEP THE ROD IN READINESS FOR A STRIKE. THIS MEANS REMOVING ALL UNNECESSARY SLACK FROM THE LINE BY THE CONTINUOUS MANEUVERING OF THE ROD-TIP. TOO MUCH SLACK WILL NEGATE EVEN THE SHARPEST REFLEXES. IN THIS CONTEXT, YOU CAN SEE WHY MOST CASTS OVER FORTY FEET ARE IN THE REALM OF CALCULATED RISK.

STREAMKEN

★ **FAMILIARITY:**
- THIS RULE OF STRATEGY STATES THAT THE MORE YOU FISH A PARTICULAR STRETCH OF WATER, THE MORE YOU'VE GOT IT WIRED AND THE MORE YOU SCORE.

★ **HOLDING WATER:**
- CERTAIN LOCATIONS ARE NATURAL HANGOUTS FOR FISH — FROM DAY TO DAY AND SEASON TO SEASON AS LONG AS THE RIVER REMAINS UN-DISTURBED BY MAN OR NATURE.

★ **HIGH WATER:**
- THE GAME USUALLY CHANGES DURING THE SPRING RUN-OFF OR AFTER A CLOUDBURST WHEN THE WATER IS HIGH AND ROILLY. SUNKEN FLIES AND BAITS WILL PROBABLY BE YOUR ONLY SALVATION.

★ **VERY LOW WATER:**
- THE FISH MIGHT HAVE MOVED TO A LESS VULNERABLE SPOT, BUT DON'T BE TOO SURE.

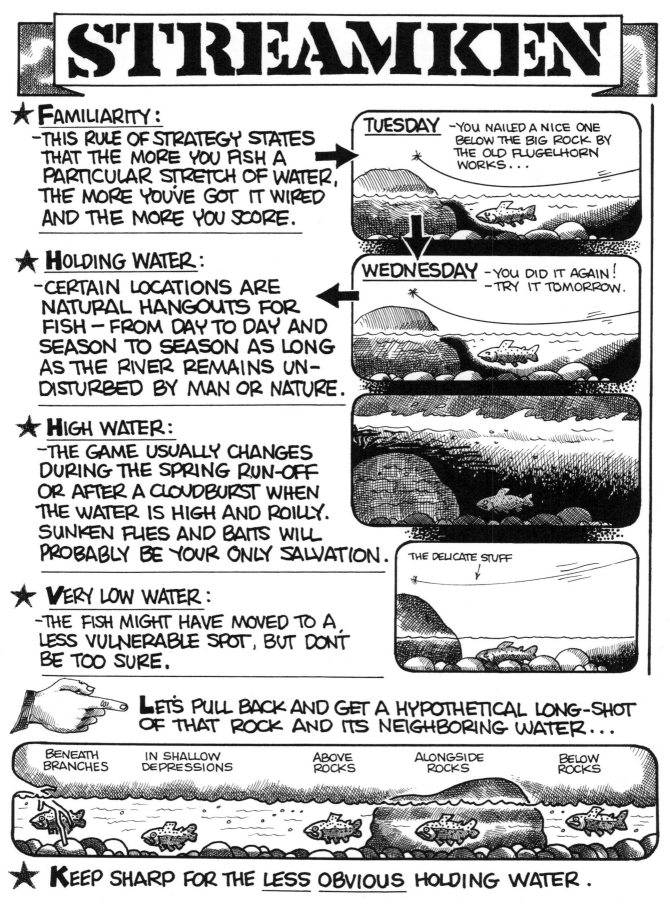

TUESDAY — YOU NAILED A NICE ONE BELOW THE BIG ROCK BY THE OLD FLUGELHORN WORKS...

WEDNESDAY — YOU DID IT AGAIN! — TRY IT TOMORROW.

THE DELICATE STUFF

LET'S PULL BACK AND GET A HYPOTHETICAL LONG-SHOT OF THAT ROCK AND ITS NEIGHBORING WATER...

| BENEATH BRANCHES | IN SHALLOW DEPRESSIONS | ABOVE ROCKS | ALONGSIDE ROCKS | BELOW ROCKS |

★ **KEEP SHARP FOR THE LESS OBVIOUS HOLDING WATER.**

READING WATER

- THE ABILITY TO TELL WHERE THE FISH ARE...

THIS IS CRUCIAL BECAUSE IF YOU DON'T KNOW WHERE THE TROUT ARE MOST LIKELY TO BE, YOU WON'T BE ABLE TO PLAN AN INTELLIGENT APPROACH. THE HOT-SPOTS ARE CALLED "HOLDING WATER"

IT'S AN ART!

① PERMANENT HOLDING WATER:

THIS IS WATER THAT AFFORDS THE TROUT A GOOD COMMAND OF THE INCOMING FOOD SUPPLY AS WELL AS CONVENIENT ACCESS TO A HIDING PLACE.

② TEMPORARY HOLDING WATER:

THIS IS WATER THE TROUT MOVE INTO STRICTLY FOR FEEDING PURPOSES, LIKE WHEN THERE'S A HATCH IN PROGRESS. THIS IS DANGEROUS WATER FOR THE TROUT BECAUSE IT'S USUALLY SHALLOW AND THERE'S NO PLACE TO HIDE. RIFFLES AND SHALLOW SIDEWATERS ARE GOOD EXAMPLES.

- IN PRAISE OF SMALL STREAMS:

IF YOU'RE A BEGINNER, I SUGGEST YOU FIND YOURSELF A GOOD CREEK AND PROCEED TO FISH EVERY METER OF IT UNTIL YOU LEARN TO RECOGNIZE THE HOT SPOTS. A CREEK IS A MINIATURE REPRESENTATION OF A RIVER BUT DOESN'T REQUIRE THE AWESOME LOGISTICS WHICH CAN CONFUSE AND BAFFLE THE NOVICE. ALSO, A CREEK DEMANDS A CERTAIN DELICACY THAT IS IMPOSSIBLE TO LEARN ON A BIG RIVER. THIS IS WHY A GOOD CREEKSMITH CAN READILY ADAPT TO A RIVER, WHILE A BIG-WATER ANGLER IS THE PROVERBIAL BULL-IN-A-CHINA-SHOPPE WHEN CONFRONTED WITH A BROOK..

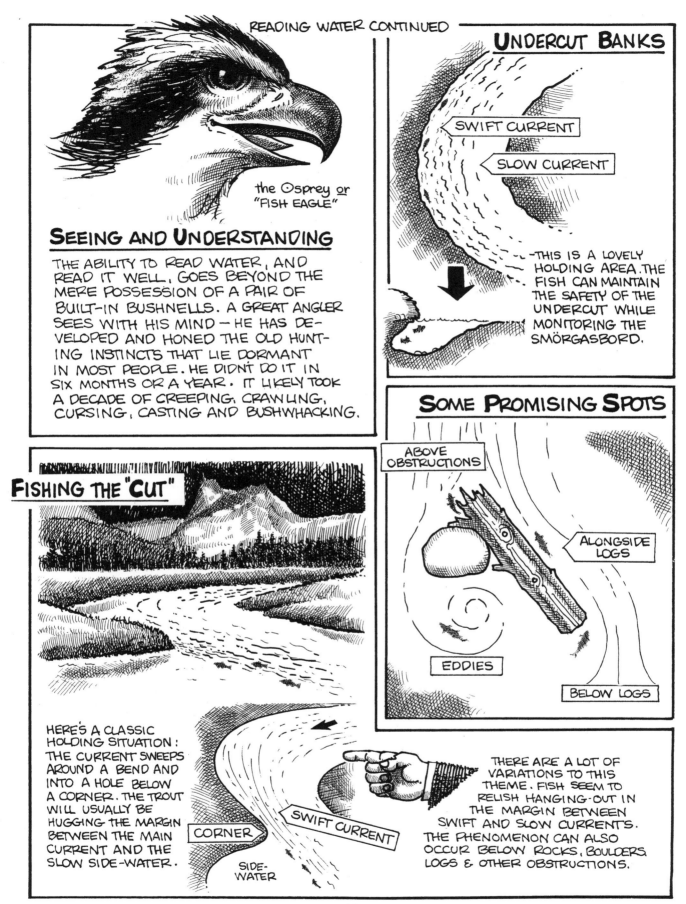

the Osprey or "FISH EAGLE"

SEEING AND UNDERSTANDING

THE ABILITY TO READ WATER, AND READ IT WELL, GOES BEYOND THE MERE POSSESSION OF A PAIR OF BUILT-IN BUSHNELLS. A GREAT ANGLER SEES WITH HIS MIND — HE HAS DEVELOPED AND HONED THE OLD HUNTING INSTINCTS THAT LIE DORMANT IN MOST PEOPLE. HE DIDN'T DO IT IN SIX MONTHS OR A YEAR. IT LIKELY TOOK A DECADE OF CREEPING, CRAWLING, CURSING, CASTING AND BUSHWHACKING.

UNDERCUT BANKS

SWIFT CURRENT

SLOW CURRENT

—THIS IS A LOVELY HOLDING AREA. THE FISH CAN MAINTAIN THE SAFETY OF THE UNDERCUT WHILE MONITORING THE SMÖRGASBORD.

FISHING THE "CUT"

SOME PROMISING SPOTS

ABOVE OBSTRUCTIONS

ALONGSIDE LOGS

EDDIES

BELOW LOGS

HERE'S A CLASSIC HOLDING SITUATION: THE CURRENT SWEEPS AROUND A BEND AND INTO A HOLE BELOW A CORNER. THE TROUT WILL USUALLY BE HUGGING THE MARGIN BETWEEN THE MAIN CURRENT AND THE SLOW SIDE-WATER.

CORNER

SWIFT CURRENT

SIDE-WATER

THERE ARE A LOT OF VARIATIONS TO THIS THEME. FISH SEEM TO RELISH HANGING-OUT IN THE MARGIN BETWEEN SWIFT AND SLOW CURRENTS. THE PHENOMENON CAN ALSO OCCUR BELOW ROCKS, BOULDERS, LOGS & OTHER OBSTRUCTIONS.

HOLES, POOLS & POCKETS

HOLES AND POOLS DENOTE THE DEEPER SLOWER-MOVING SECTIONS OF A RIVER OR STREAM. THE DEFINITIONS ARE RELATIVE — FOR INSTANCE, A FOOT-DEEP POCKET ON A RIVER MIGHT BE A DEEP-POOL IF INSTALLED ON A TINY BROOK.

ALWAYS BE AWARE OF THE POSITION OF THE SUN IN RELATION TO THE INTENDED APPROACH. EVEN THE SHADOW OF YOUR ROD-TIP ON THE TARGET-WATER WILL SCARE THE FISH.

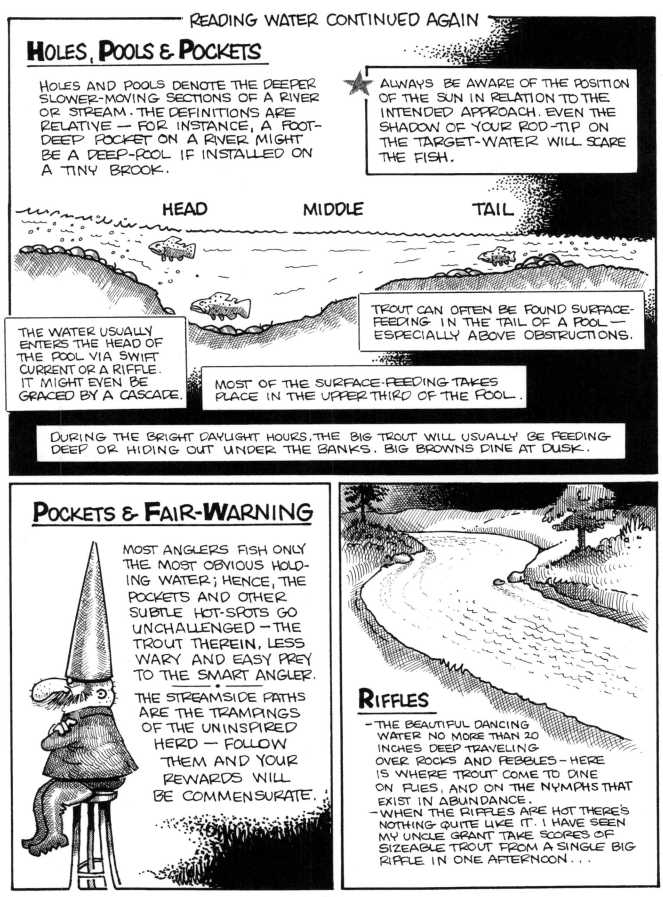

HEAD   MIDDLE   TAIL

TROUT CAN OFTEN BE FOUND SURFACE-FEEDING IN THE TAIL OF A POOL — ESPECIALLY ABOVE OBSTRUCTIONS.

THE WATER USUALLY ENTERS THE HEAD OF THE POOL VIA SWIFT CURRENT OR A RIFFLE. IT MIGHT EVEN BE GRACED BY A CASCADE.

MOST OF THE SURFACE-FEEDING TAKES PLACE IN THE UPPER THIRD OF THE POOL.

DURING THE BRIGHT DAYLIGHT HOURS, THE BIG TROUT WILL USUALLY BE FEEDING DEEP OR HIDING OUT UNDER THE BANKS. BIG BROWNS DINE AT DUSK.

POCKETS & FAIR-WARNING

MOST ANGLERS FISH ONLY THE MOST OBVIOUS HOLD-ING WATER; HENCE, THE POCKETS AND OTHER SUBTLE HOT-SPOTS GO UNCHALLENGED — THE TROUT THEREIN, LESS WARY AND EASY PREY TO THE SMART ANGLER.

THE STREAMSIDE PATHS ARE THE TRAMPINGS OF THE UNINSPIRED HERD — FOLLOW THEM AND YOUR REWARDS WILL BE COMMENSURATE.

RIFFLES

- THE BEAUTIFUL DANCING WATER NO MORE THAN 20 INCHES DEEP TRAVELING OVER ROCKS AND PEBBLES — HERE IS WHERE TROUT COME TO DINE ON FLIES, AND ON THE NYMPHS THAT EXIST IN ABUNDANCE.
- WHEN THE RIFFLES ARE HOT THERE'S NOTHING QUITE LIKE IT. I HAVE SEEN MY UNCLE GRANT TAKE SCORES OF SIZEABLE TROUT FROM A SINGLE BIG RIFFLE IN ONE AFTERNOON . . .

HIDDEN SHELVES

NEAR BRIDGES & DAMS

ENTRANCE TO SIDE-STREAM

A WORD ABOUT SIDE-STREAMS

—MANY TIMES I'VE FOUND THAT A FIFTEEN OR TWENTY MINUTE STROLL UP A SIDE-STREAM OR CREEK WILL YIELD THE BEST FISHING OF THE DAY. THIS IS BECAUSE THE MAJORITY OF THE WORLD'S HACKLE-JOCKEYS TEND TO SNEER AT THE SMALLER WATERS, DEEMING THEM UNWORTHY OF THEIR SKILLS — MAY THEY ALWAYS CHERISH THAT DELUSION.

IN SHADOWS

NO TRESPASSING

POCKETS & SIDEWATERS IN RAPIDS

THERE'S MORE TO WHITE-WATER THAN MOST FISHERS THINK. DON'T PASS IT UP WITHOUT A TRY.

BELOW ISLANDS

IN MOSS

AN ABUNDANCE OF MOSS INDICATES A LOT OF FEED AND CONSEQUENTLY A LOT OF FISH. THE PROBLEM IS THAT THE FISH WILL TEND TO BE FUSSY ABOUT THEIR DIET.

STONEFLY

DAMSEL FLY

STONEFLY NYMPH

DAMSEL FLY NYMPH

MIDGE PUPA

CADDIS FLY

MIDGE

CADDIS LARVA WITHOUT CASE

SPITFIRE

DRAGON FLY NYMPH

ANT

MAYFLY NYMPH

CRICKET

GRASSHOPPER

MAYFLY

YOUR FRIENDLY LOCAL EMPIRICIST

TROUT EAT ALL KINDS OF BUGS; HENCE, I RECOMMEND THAT YOU ACQUAINT YOURSELF WITH THE ENTOMOLOGY OF YOUR OWN WATERS SO YOU CAN MAKE AN INTELLIGENT FLY SELECTION.

I KNOW A GUY WHO RAISES NYMPHS IN HIS OWN HOME. HE'S GOT A SOPHISTICATED AQUARIUM SETUP IN HIS LIVING ROOM, AND WHILE THE REST OF US ARE SNAKED-OUT ON LUCKY-LAGER AND THE MONDAY-NITE MOVIE, THIS DUDE IS ZEROING IN ON THE BEHAVIOR OF AQUATIC INSECTS.

WITH SUCH DEDICATION AND INGENUITY, IT'S NOT SURPRISING THAT THIS ANGLER CATCHES MORE FISH THAN A RUSSIAN TRAWLER — FORTUNATELY, HE RELEASES MOST OF THEM. I'VE SEEN HIM RETURN SPECIMENS THAT I WOULD JOYOUSLY HAVE DRAGGED AROUND THE GATES OF TROY.

HIS WIFE IS IN ON IT TOO. SHE'S AN ACCOMPLISHED PHOTOGRAPHER AND TAKES EXQUISITE CLOSE-UP SLIDES OF ALMOST EVERY IMAGINABLE TERRESTRIAL & AQUATIC BUG. MOST OF HER SHOOTING IS DONE ON LOCATION, UTILIZING AN IMPRESSIVE ARSENAL OF SCREENS, NETS, AND COLLECTING DEVICES.

NOT MANY ANGLERS WILL BE INCLINED TO PURSUE THE STUDY OF BUGS TO THIS EXTREME, BUT I BELIEVE THAT THE SERIOUS FLY FISHER SHOULD EMBRACE ENTOMOLOGY AS AN INTEGRAL PART OF THE FISHING EXPERIENCE.

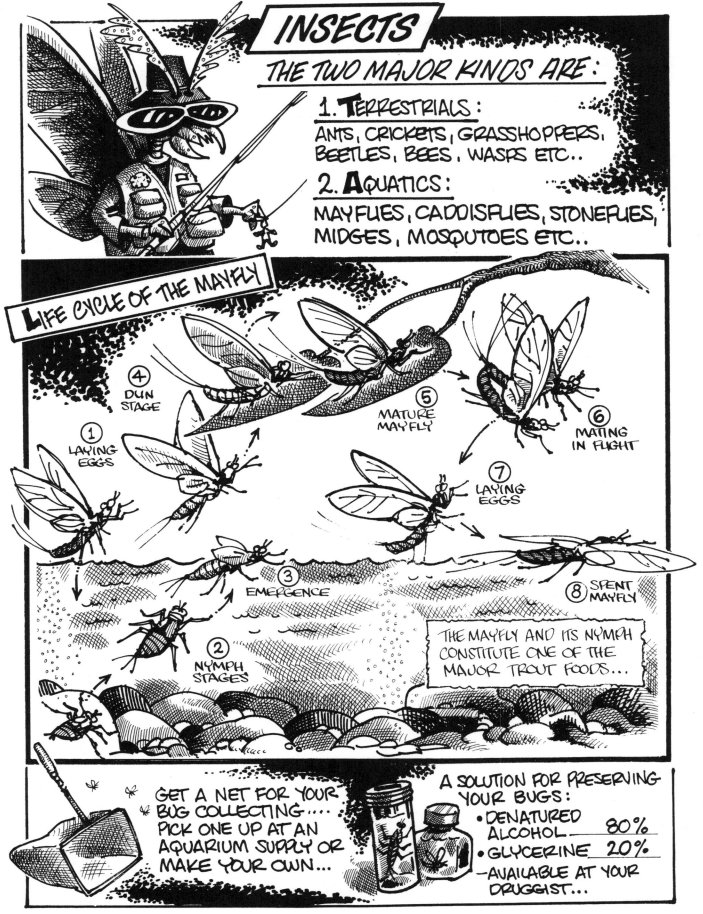

INSECTS
THE TWO MAJOR KINDS ARE:

1. TERRESTRIALS:
ANTS, CRICKETS, GRASSHOPPERS, BEETLES, BEES, WASPS ETC..

2. AQUATICS:
MAYFLIES, CADDISFLIES, STONEFLIES, MIDGES, MOSQUITOES ETC...

LIFE CYCLE OF THE MAYFLY

④ DUN STAGE

① LAYING EGGS

⑤ MATURE MAYFLY

⑥ MATING IN FLIGHT

⑦ LAYING EGGS

③ EMERGENCE

② NYMPH STAGES

⑧ SPENT MAYFLY

THE MAYFLY AND ITS NYMPH CONSTITUTE ONE OF THE MAJOR TROUT FOODS...

GET A NET FOR YOUR BUG COLLECTING.... PICK ONE UP AT AN AQUARIUM SUPPLY OR MAKE YOUR OWN...

A SOLUTION FOR PRESERVING YOUR BUGS:
- DENATURED ALCOHOL ___ 80%
- GLYCERINE ___ 20%
- AVAILABLE AT YOUR DRUGGIST...

NYMPHS

THE CRUCIAL PROBLEM WITH NYMPHS AND WETS IS THE DIFFICULTY OF DETERMINING THE MOMENT OF STRIKE — THE UNDULATING WATER-SURFACE CAN BAFFLE THE KEENEST SET OF EYES. SO YOU'VE GOT TO BE EXTREMELY ALERT. OFTEN YOUR ONLY INDICATION WILL BE A DIM FLASH AS THE FISH TURNS TO TAKE THE FLY. KEEP SHARP FOR UNUSUAL MOVEMENT OR HALTING OF THE LINE & LEADER — FOR THIS, YOU MIGHT APPRECIATE AN "INDICATOR".

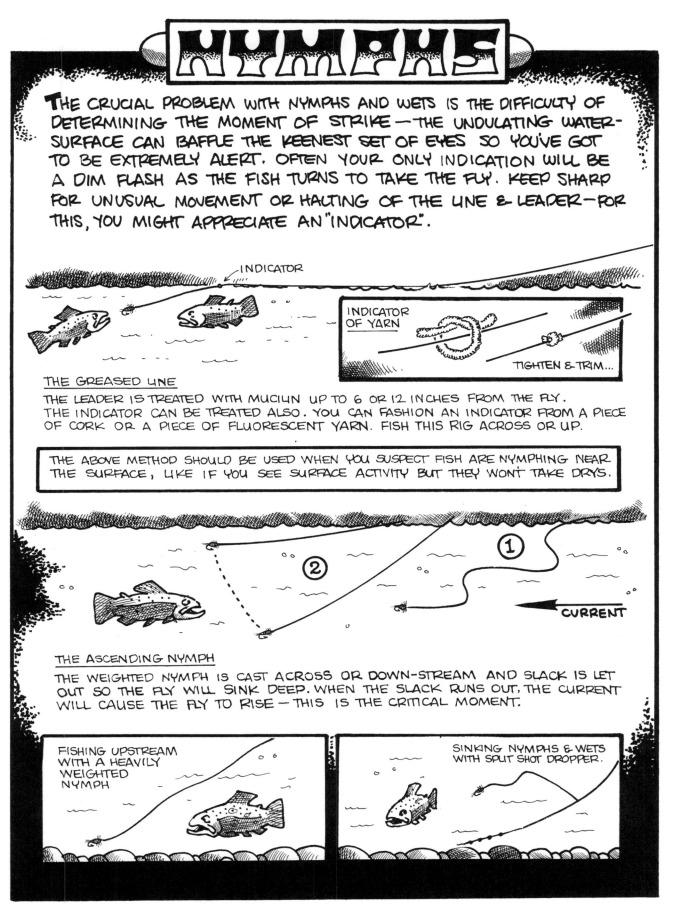

INDICATOR

INDICATOR
OF YARN

TIGHTEN & TRIM...

THE GREASED LINE

THE LEADER IS TREATED WITH MUCILIN UP TO 6 OR 12 INCHES FROM THE FLY. THE INDICATOR CAN BE TREATED ALSO. YOU CAN FASHION AN INDICATOR FROM A PIECE OF CORK OR A PIECE OF FLUORESCENT YARN. FISH THIS RIG ACROSS OR UP.

THE ABOVE METHOD SHOULD BE USED WHEN YOU SUSPECT FISH ARE NYMPHING NEAR THE SURFACE, LIKE IF YOU SEE SURFACE ACTIVITY BUT THEY WON'T TAKE DRYS.

② ①

CURRENT

THE ASCENDING NYMPH

THE WEIGHTED NYMPH IS CAST ACROSS OR DOWN-STREAM AND SLACK IS LET OUT SO THE FLY WILL SINK DEEP. WHEN THE SLACK RUNS OUT, THE CURRENT WILL CAUSE THE FLY TO RISE — THIS IS THE CRITICAL MOMENT.

FISHING UPSTREAM WITH A HEAVILY WEIGHTED NYMPH

SINKING NYMPHS & WETS WITH SPLIT SHOT DROPPER.

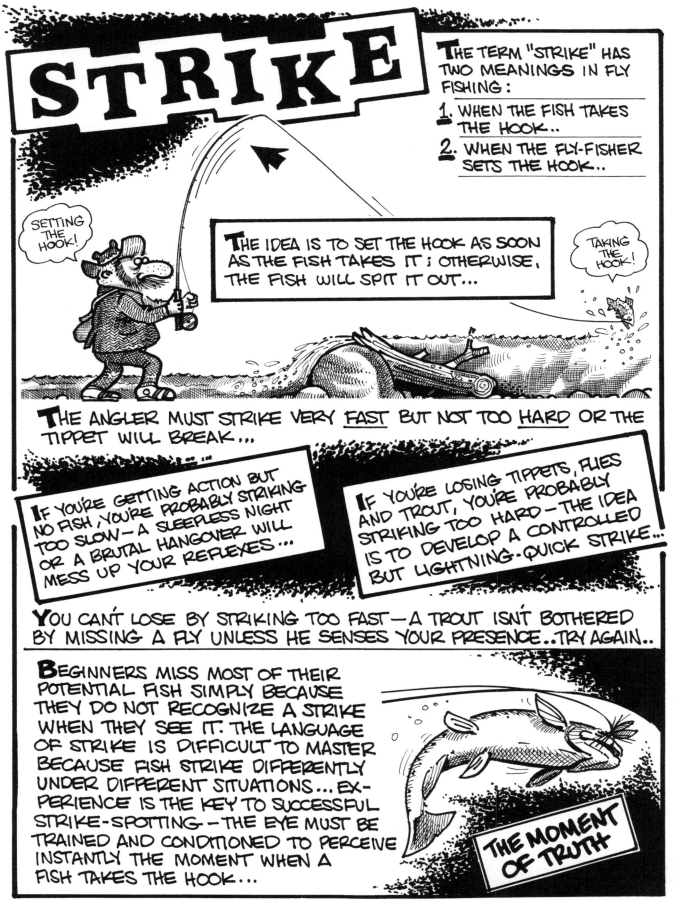

STRIKE

THE TERM "STRIKE" HAS TWO MEANINGS IN FLY FISHING:

1. WHEN THE FISH TAKES THE HOOK...
2. WHEN THE FLY-FISHER SETS THE HOOK...

SETTING THE HOOK!

THE IDEA IS TO SET THE HOOK AS SOON AS THE FISH TAKES IT; OTHERWISE, THE FISH WILL SPIT IT OUT...

TAKING THE HOOK!

THE ANGLER MUST STRIKE VERY FAST BUT NOT TOO HARD OR THE TIPPET WILL BREAK...

IF YOU'RE GETTING ACTION BUT NO FISH, YOU'RE PROBABLY STRIKING TOO SLOW — A SLEEPLESS NIGHT OR A BRUTAL HANGOVER WILL MESS UP YOUR REFLEXES...

IF YOU'RE LOSING TIPPETS, FLIES AND TROUT, YOU'RE PROBABLY STRIKING TOO HARD — THE IDEA IS TO DEVELOP A CONTROLLED BUT LIGHTNING-QUICK STRIKE...

YOU CAN'T LOSE BY STRIKING TOO FAST — A TROUT ISN'T BOTHERED BY MISSING A FLY UNLESS HE SENSES YOUR PRESENCE.. TRY AGAIN..

BEGINNERS MISS MOST OF THEIR POTENTIAL FISH SIMPLY BECAUSE THEY DO NOT RECOGNIZE A STRIKE WHEN THEY SEE IT. THE LANGUAGE OF STRIKE IS DIFFICULT TO MASTER BECAUSE FISH STRIKE DIFFERENTLY UNDER DIFFERENT SITUATIONS... EXPERIENCE IS THE KEY TO SUCCESSFUL STRIKE-SPOTTING — THE EYE MUST BE TRAINED AND CONDITIONED TO PERCEIVE INSTANTLY THE MOMENT WHEN A FISH TAKES THE HOOK...

THE MOMENT OF TRUTH

PLAYING

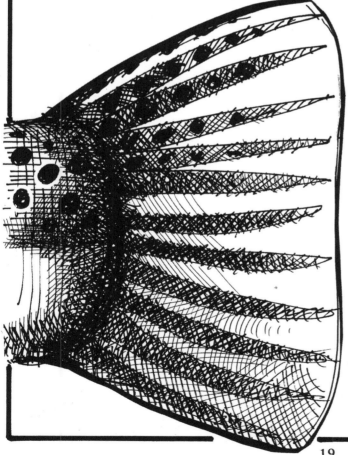

THE AVERAGE TROUT IS VERY FORGIVING, A LITTLE COMMON SENSE AND HE'S YOURS; BUT WHEN THE CREATURE APPROACHES THE 20 INCH NOTCH THE CARDS ARE STACKED AGAINST YOU... HERE ARE A FEW GUIDELINES TO HELP KEEP YOU FROM SINGING THE BYE-BYE BLUES:

DON'T, DON'T, DON'T TRY TO CHECK THE FIRST EXPLOSIVE RUN. GIVE THE WRETCHED ANIMAL ALL THE LINE IT WANTS AND GIVE IT FAST. CHANCES ARE THE ABSENCE OF RESISTANCE WILL CAUSE THE BEAST TO HALT WELL WITHIN THE LIMITS OF LINE AND BACKING.. REMEMBER: THE HARDER YOU PULL – THE HARDER THE FISH WILL PULL. YOU DON'T NEED TO BE A MATHEMATICIAN TO FIGURE THE ODDS ON A BROKEN TIPPET. KEEP THE PRESSURE OFF UNTIL THE HEAVY FIREWORKS SUBSIDE...

TRY AND KEEP THE MONSTER OBLIVIOUS TO YOUR PRESENCE. GET OUT OF SIGHT OR REMAIN STILL WHILE PLAYING. ATTEMPT TO GET BELOW THE FISH AT YOUR FIRST OPPORTUNITY.

A PERSISTENT <u>SIDEWAY'S</u> PRESSURE WILL EVENTUALLY TIRE THE FISH. TRY TO STEER THE TROUT INTO THE SLOWER SIDEWATERS SO YOU WON'T BE FIGHTING BOTH FISH AND CURRENT...

DON'T GET ANTSY AND ATTEMPT TO HORSE THE FISH IN. WAIT UNTIL HE GOES OVER ON HIS SIDE THEN BEGIN WORKING HIM TOWARD THE SHORE OR YOUR NET...

IT'S LOSING THE BIG ONES THAT WILL HASTEN YOU TO THE MADHOUSE – A COOL HEAD WILL HELP KEEP THE STRAIGHT-JACKET AT BAY...

NEXT PAGE

LARGE FISH CAN BEST BE PLAYED WITH THE ROD HELD IN THE LEFT HAND. THIS LEAVES THE RIGHT HAND FREE FOR FEEDING OUT LINE AND REELING IN...

LANDING

HERE, THE WHITE-CRESTED CLACKAMAS CUCKOO DEMONSTRATES THE ART OF NETTING. NOTE THE POSITION OF THE ROD IN RELATION TO THE NET; THE ALGERIAN BRIAR IN RELATION TO THE BEAK...

BEACHING A FISH

TROUT CAN ALSO BE LANDED BY GENTLY GRASPING ABOUT THE MIDDLE. EASY DOES IT...

KILLING

IF YOU INSIST ON KEEPING A FISH YOU SHOULD BE HUMANE AND GIVE IT A SWIFT AND MERCIFUL DEATH...

KILLING
RAP THE HEAD SHARPLY AGAINST A ROCK OR TREE.

KILL IN MIDSTREAM BY BEANING THE FISH ON THE RIM OF LANDING NET — OR CARRY A STICK.

CATCH AND RELEASE

FLY FISHING IS THE CLASSIEST CHESS GAME IN TOWN AND WE MUST BE CHIVALROUS ENOUGH TO LEAVE THE PIECES ON THE BOARD SO THAT OTHERS CAN PLAY — CATCH AND RELEASE IS THE ONLY WAY TO INSURE THE QUALITY OF THE SPORT...

RELEASING
HOLD GENTLY 'TIL THE FISH CAN SWIM AWAY. DONT INJURE WHEN LANDING.

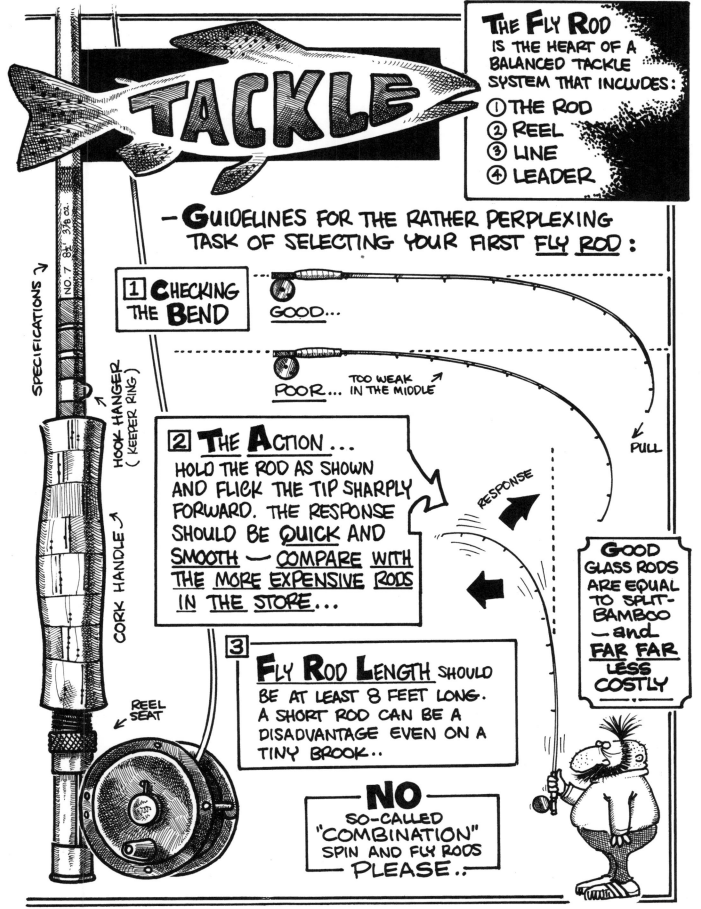

TACKLE

THE FLY ROD IS THE HEART OF A BALANCED TACKLE SYSTEM THAT INCLUDES:
1. THE ROD
2. REEL
3. LINE
4. LEADER

— GUIDELINES FOR THE RATHER PERPLEXING TASK OF SELECTING YOUR FIRST FLY ROD:

1 CHECKING THE BEND

GOOD...

POOR... TOO WEAK IN THE MIDDLE

PULL

2 THE ACTION... HOLD THE ROD AS SHOWN AND FLICK THE TIP SHARPLY FORWARD. THE RESPONSE SHOULD BE QUICK AND SMOOTH — COMPARE WITH THE MORE EXPENSIVE RODS IN THE STORE...

RESPONSE

3 FLY ROD LENGTH SHOULD BE AT LEAST 8 FEET LONG. A SHORT ROD CAN BE A DISADVANTAGE EVEN ON A TINY BROOK..

GOOD GLASS RODS ARE EQUAL TO SPLIT-BAMBOO — and FAR FAR LESS COSTLY

NO SO-CALLED "COMBINATION" SPIN AND FLY RODS PLEASE..

SPECIFICATIONS

NO. 7 8½' 3⅞ OZ.

HOOK HANGER (KEEPER RING)

CORK HANDLE

REEL SEAT

THE REEL THING

THERE ARE TWO BASIC TYPES OF FLY REELS, THE "AUTOMATIC" AND THE "SINGLE ACTION"... THE SINGLE ACTION IS YOUR BEST BET BECAUSE —

A. IT'S SIMPLER...
B. GREATER LINE CAPACITY...
C. EASIER TO MAINTAIN...
D. IS LIGHTER...
E. WIDER RANGE OF USE...
F. BUILDS CHARACTER...

SINGLE ACTION REEL
(RIGHT HANDED)

THE REEL MUST HAVE ENOUGH CAPACITY TO COMFORTABLY CONTAIN A DOUBLE TAPERED FLOATING FLY LINE AND A MINIMUM OF THIRTY YARDS OF 20 POUND TEST BRAIDED DACRON BACKING... (-100 YARDS FOR STEELHEAD.) SEE BOTTOM OF THIS PAGE..)

6"

THE ROD AND REEL SHOULD PHYSICALLY BALANCE SOMEWHERE WITHIN THE DOTTED LINES AS SHOWN...

FLY REEL

MOST MANUFACTURERS PROVIDE CAPACITY SPECIFICATIONS AND MAINTENANCE INFORMATION WITH EACH REEL SOLD...

CHECK INSIDE THE BOX FOR A SMALL BROCHURE...

ADJUSTABLE DRAG

A GADGET USUALLY FOUND ON FANCIER REELS.. USEFUL FOR PLAYING LARGE FISH BUT NOT REALLY NECESSARY FOR MOST SITUATIONS...

AUTOMATICS

-AUTOMATIC REELS ARE ACTIVATED BY A STEEL SPRING AND A CLUTCH DEVICE... DROP ONE IN A SANDY CREEK AND LEARN SOMETHING ABOUT APPLIED MECHANICS...

BACKING — IS SIMPLY

AN EXTENSION OF YOUR LINE WHICH PROVIDES THE EXTRA LENGTH NEEDED TO PLAY A LARGE FISH ... IT CAN BEST BE APPRECIATED ON THOSE RARE OCCASIONS WHEN YOU HOOK A TROUT OF ROUGHLY THE SAME TONNAGE AS YOUR FORELEG AND THE UNRULY BEAST IS MOVING RELENTLESSLY IN THE DIRECTION OF THE NEXT COUNTY ...

← REEL   BACKING ↘   ↙ DOUBLE TAPERED LINE

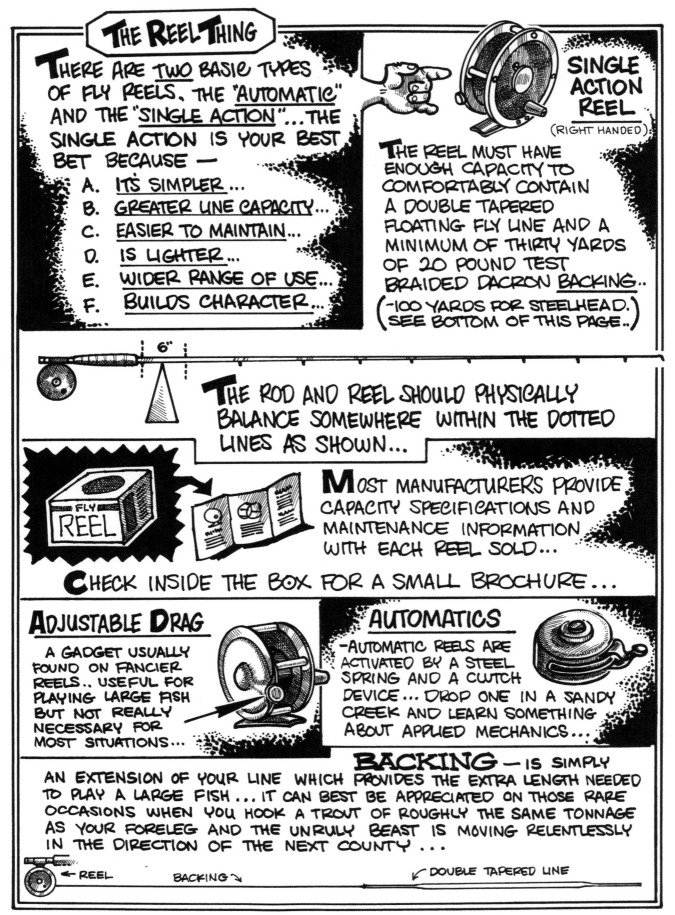

FLY LINE

An outfit called "AFTMA" (The American Fishing Tackle Manufacturers Association) has set-up a line standardization system that makes selection virtually painless...

-Each rod manufacturer gives a recommended AFTMA line weight No. for every rod...

SO

-If the manufacturer recommends a #6 line, you purchase a "DT-6-F" line...

The "DT" means Double-Tapered and the "F" means Floating... a double tapered, floating line is the most effective for general use...

Diagram of a double tapered line...

| 2' | 11' | 65' | 11' | 2' |
| TAPER | | BELLY | TAPER | |

Although initially expensive, the double tapered line is the most economical because when one end becomes a bit frayed, you can reverse it...

The better to keep tabs on your fly, choose a light colored fly line...

White's OK too!

If someone lays a vintage fly rod on you, lug it on down to the local tackle shoppe and COMPARE in order to determine correct line...

AFTMA wt. is based on the first 30 feet of line

Weight recommendations are not absolute... reducing line wt. by one number will give you better handling with only a minimal loss of casting distance...

AFTMA WEIGHT NO.	WEIGHT IN GRAINS	WEIGHT LENGTH
4	120	30'
5	140	30'
6	160	30'
7	185	30'
8	210	30'
9	240	30'
10	280	30'

LEADER

There are TWO kinds of TAPERED LEADERS:
1. HAND-TIED
2. KNOTLESS

Basically, the leader is a length of transparent monofilament nylon that acts as a sort of invisible link between the fly-line and the fly...

Every self respecting all-purpose fly leader should be properly TAPERED., a good taper allows the energy from the line to flow smoothly into the leader so that it turns over and sets the fly GENTLY upon the water...

Hand tied leaders are a bit tricky for the beginner so I suggest that you start out with a knotless, which can be purchased at the tackle shoppe for less than the price of a shot of whiskey..

CATCH 22!

The finer the tippet the better to fool the fish.....
But, the finer the tippet the easier it breaks!

Diagram of Tapered Leaders

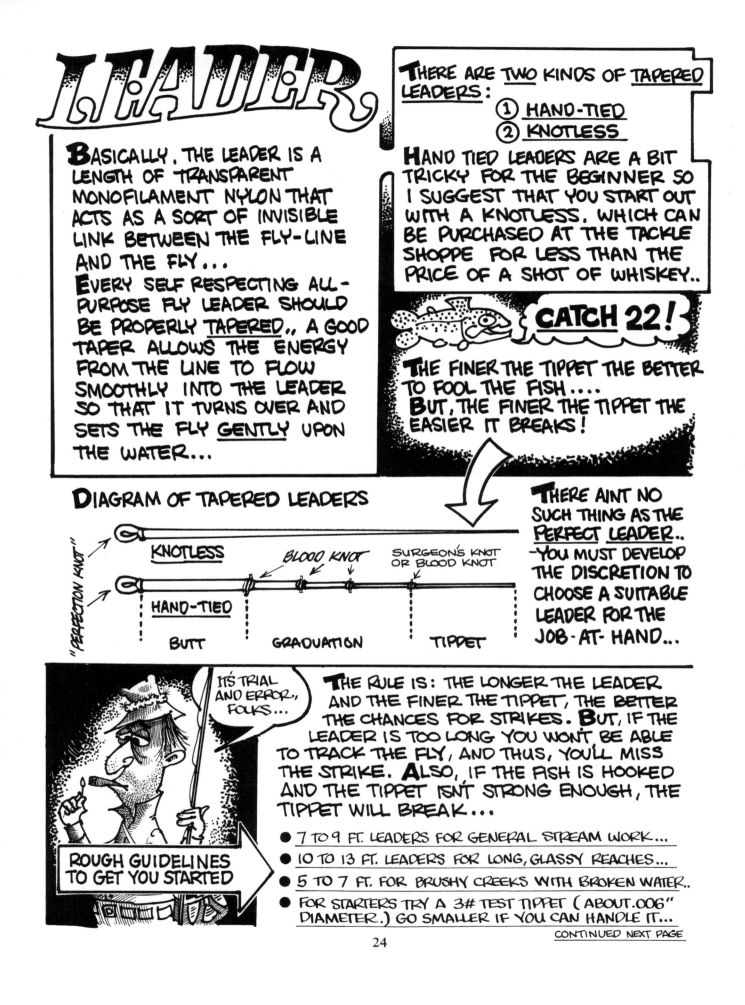

"PERFECTION KNOT"

KNOTLESS

HAND-TIED

BLOOD KNOT

SURGEON'S KNOT OR BLOOD KNOT

BUTT   GRADUATION   TIPPET

There aint no such thing as the PERFECT LEADER.. -You must develop the discretion to choose a suitable leader for the job-at-hand...

IT'S TRIAL AND ERROR, FOLKS...

ROUGH GUIDELINES TO GET YOU STARTED

The rule is: the longer the leader and the finer the tippet, the better the chances for strikes. But, if the leader is too long you won't be able to track the fly, and thus, you'll miss the strike. Also, if the fish is hooked and the tippet isn't strong enough, the tippet will break...

- 7 to 9 ft. leaders for general stream work...
- 10 to 13 ft. leaders for long, glassy reaches...
- 5 to 7 ft. for brushy creeks with broken water..
- For starters try a 3# test tippet (about .006" diameter.) go smaller if you can handle it...

CONTINUED NEXT PAGE

"LINE END SYSTEM"

THIS IS SIMPLY A HEAVY PIECE OF LEADER MATERIAL ABOUT 8 INCHES LONG ATTACHED PERMANENTLY TO THE LINE WHICH ENABLES YOU TO CHANGE LEADERS QUICKLY AND EASILY. IT SHOULD BE SLIGHTLY LESS IN DIAMETER THAN THE LINE END - PROBABLY ABOUT .020" DIAMETER OR AROUND 25-POUND TEST....

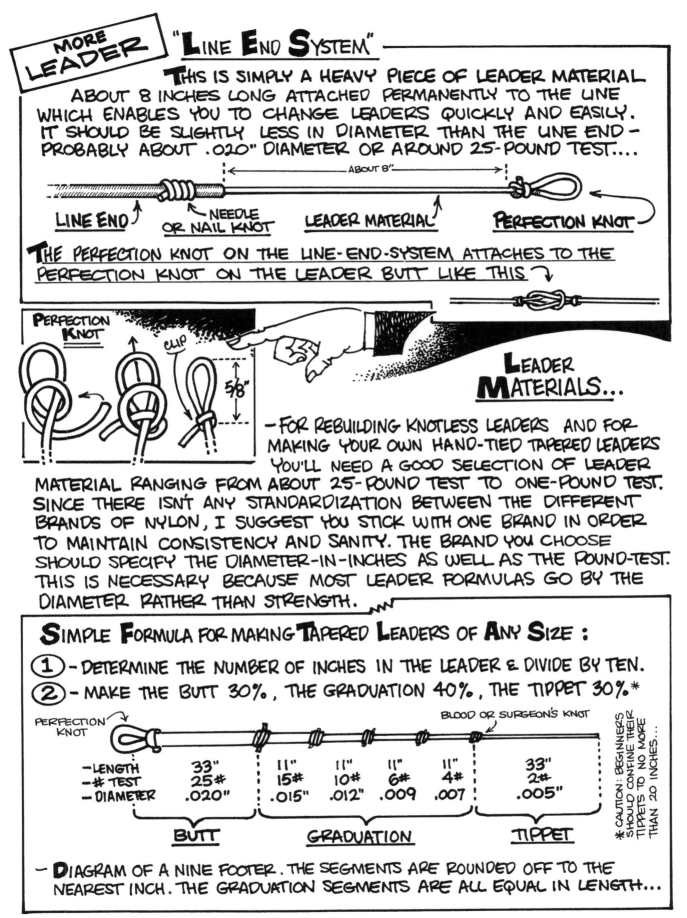

LINE END — NEEDLE OR NAIL KNOT — LEADER MATERIAL — PERFECTION KNOT — ABOUT 8"

THE PERFECTION KNOT ON THE LINE-END-SYSTEM ATTACHES TO THE PERFECTION KNOT ON THE LEADER BUTT LIKE THIS ↓

PERFECTION KNOT — CLIP — 5/8"

LEADER MATERIALS...

– FOR REBUILDING KNOTLESS LEADERS AND FOR MAKING YOUR OWN HAND-TIED TAPERED LEADERS YOU'LL NEED A GOOD SELECTION OF LEADER MATERIAL RANGING FROM ABOUT 25-POUND TEST TO ONE-POUND TEST. SINCE THERE ISN'T ANY STANDARDIZATION BETWEEN THE DIFFERENT BRANDS OF NYLON, I SUGGEST YOU STICK WITH ONE BRAND IN ORDER TO MAINTAIN CONSISTENCY AND SANITY. THE BRAND YOU CHOOSE SHOULD SPECIFY THE DIAMETER-IN-INCHES AS WELL AS THE POUND-TEST. THIS IS NECESSARY BECAUSE MOST LEADER FORMULAS GO BY THE DIAMETER RATHER THAN STRENGTH.

SIMPLE FORMULA FOR MAKING TAPERED LEADERS OF ANY SIZE :

① – DETERMINE THE NUMBER OF INCHES IN THE LEADER & DIVIDE BY TEN.

② – MAKE THE BUTT 30%, THE GRADUATION 40%, THE TIPPET 30%.*

PERFECTION KNOT — BLOOD OR SURGEON'S KNOT

	BUTT	GRADUATION				TIPPET
–LENGTH	33"	11"	11"	11"	11"	33"
–# TEST	25#	15#	10#	6#	4#	2#
–DIAMETER	.020"	.015"	.012"	.009	.007	.005"

* CAUTION: BEGINNERS SHOULD CONFINE THEIR TIPPETS TO NO MORE THAN 20 INCHES....

– DIAGRAM OF A NINE FOOTER. THE SEGMENTS ARE ROUNDED OFF TO THE NEAREST INCH. THE GRADUATION SEGMENTS ARE ALL EQUAL IN LENGTH...

FLIES and TOOFARAW

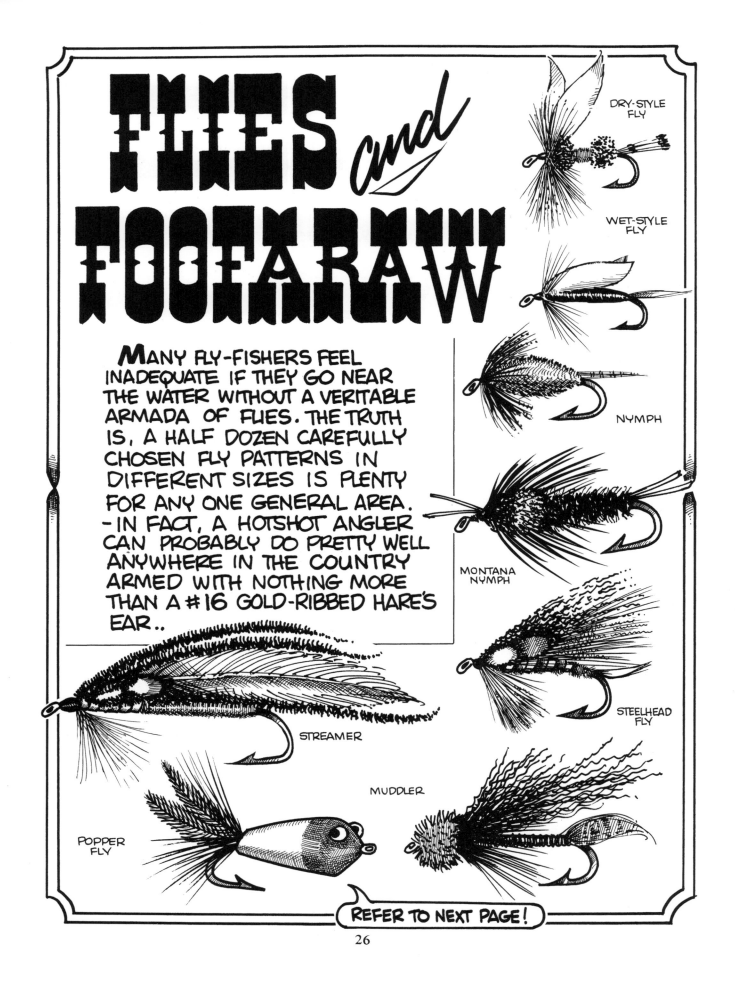

MANY FLY-FISHERS FEEL INADEQUATE IF THEY GO NEAR THE WATER WITHOUT A VERITABLE ARMADA OF FLIES. THE TRUTH IS, A HALF DOZEN CAREFULLY CHOSEN FLY PATTERNS IN DIFFERENT SIZES IS PLENTY FOR ANY ONE GENERAL AREA. —IN FACT, A HOTSHOT ANGLER CAN PROBABLY DO PRETTY WELL ANYWHERE IN THE COUNTRY ARMED WITH NOTHING MORE THAN A #16 GOLD-RIBBED HARE'S EAR..

DRY-STYLE FLY

WET-STYLE FLY

NYMPH

MONTANA NYMPH

STEELHEAD FLY

STREAMER

MUDDLER

POPPER FLY

REFER TO NEXT PAGE!

THE TERMS WET AND DRY REFER TO THE STYLE IN WHICH A FLY IS TIED... THEY ALSO INDICATE WHETHER A FLY IS FISHED SUNKEN, OR FLOATING ON THE SURFACE... FOR INSTANCE, A DRY-STYLE FLY CAN BE FISHED WET—AND VICE-VERSA...

DRY FLIES

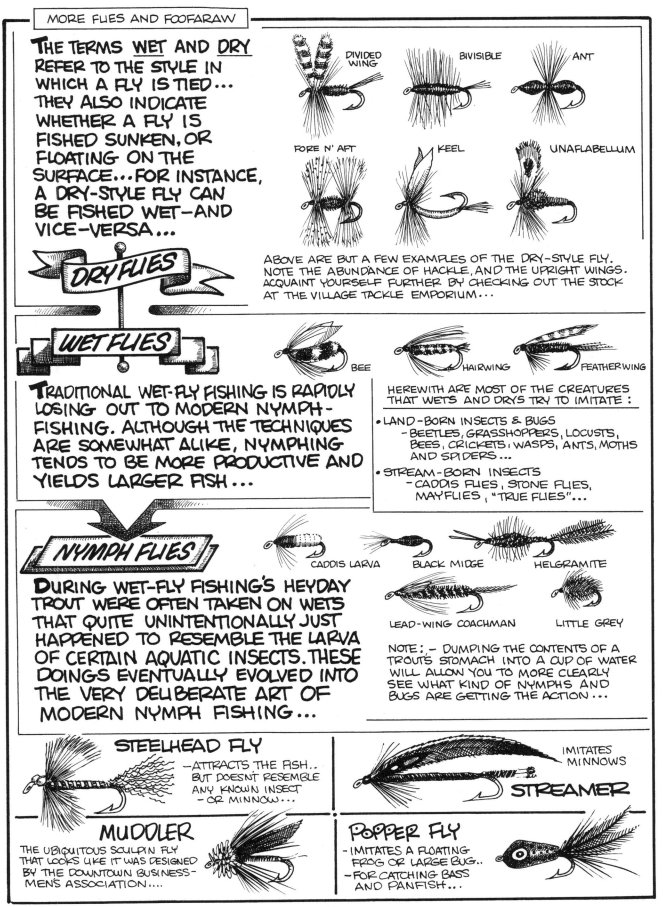

DIVIDED WING

BIVISIBLE

ANT

FORE N' AFT

KEEL

UNAFLABELLUM

ABOVE ARE BUT A FEW EXAMPLES OF THE DRY-STYLE FLY. NOTE THE ABUNDANCE OF HACKLE, AND THE UPRIGHT WINGS. ACQUAINT YOURSELF FURTHER BY CHECKING OUT THE STOCK AT THE VILLAGE TACKLE EMPORIUM...

WET FLIES

BEE

HAIRWING

FEATHERWING

TRADITIONAL WET-FLY FISHING IS RAPIDLY LOSING OUT TO MODERN NYMPH-FISHING. ALTHOUGH THE TECHNIQUES ARE SOMEWHAT ALIKE, NYMPHING TENDS TO BE MORE PRODUCTIVE AND YIELDS LARGER FISH...

HEREWITH ARE MOST OF THE CREATURES THAT WETS AND DRYS TRY TO IMITATE:

• LAND-BORN INSECTS & BUGS
  - BEETLES, GRASSHOPPERS, LOCUSTS, BEES, CRICKETS, WASPS, ANTS, MOTHS AND SPIDERS...
• STREAM-BORN INSECTS
  - CADDIS FLIES, STONE FLIES, MAYFLIES, "TRUE FLIES"...

NYMPH FLIES

CADDIS LARVA

BLACK MIDGE

HELGRAMITE

LEAD-WING COACHMAN

LITTLE GREY

DURING WET-FLY FISHING'S HEYDAY TROUT WERE OFTEN TAKEN ON WETS THAT QUITE UNINTENTIONALLY JUST HAPPENED TO RESEMBLE THE LARVA OF CERTAIN AQUATIC INSECTS. THESE DOINGS EVENTUALLY EVOLVED INTO THE VERY DELIBERATE ART OF MODERN NYMPH FISHING...

NOTE:— DUMPING THE CONTENTS OF A TROUT'S STOMACH INTO A CUP OF WATER WILL ALLOW YOU TO MORE CLEARLY SEE WHAT KIND OF NYMPHS AND BUGS ARE GETTING THE ACTION...

STEELHEAD FLY
—ATTRACTS THE FISH.. BUT DOESN'T RESEMBLE ANY KNOWN INSECT - OR MINNOW...

IMITATES MINNOWS

STREAMER

MUDDLER
THE UBIQUITOUS SCULPIN FLY THAT LOOKS LIKE IT WAS DESIGNED BY THE DOWNTOWN BUSINESS-MEN'S ASSOCIATION....

POPPER FLY
- IMITATES A FLOATING FROG OR LARGE BUG..
- FOR CATCHING BASS AND PANFISH...

GEAR

CREEL — These wicker jobs are classic but canvas is best for brush and for backpacking..

"YER OL' GREY BONNET, WITH ALL THE JUNK UPON-IT.."

LANDING NET

FLY BOX

LEADER KIT...

MOSQUITO DOPE

TAPERED LEADER STORAGE BOX

POLAROIDS — sometimes very handy — sometimes not....

POCKET KNIFE

— TRADITIONAL COSTUME OF THE FLY ANGLER....
— NOTE THE STEELY GAZE AND THE IMPERIOUS AYRE...

LUCKY FISHIN' HAT

POLAROID GLASSES

LICENSE

CREEL

LANDING NET

STIFF UPPER LIP

CAMOUFLAGE CLOTHING

HIP BOOTS

PEN-LIGHT FOR TYING KNOTS & FINDING CAMP..

GYM-SHOES — INSTEAD OF BOOTS & WADERS..

"BURRRR!"

A TINY DAB ON THE FLY MAKES IT FLOAT BETTER...GOOD FOR LINES ALSO.."MUCILIN"

MUCILIN

Hooks · Knots

THE FIRST ACTUAL FISH HOOKS WERE MADE DURING THE LATE STONE AGE... THESE NEOLITHIC TOOLS WERE FASHIONED FROM BONE. MANY LOOKED LIKE THIS:

HOOK SIZES VARY FROM ONE BRAND TO ANOTHER...
THEY ARE AVAILABLE IN A LARGE VARIETY OF STYLES FOR A VARIETY OF DIFFERENT USES & SITUATIONS...

SALMON EGG
BAIT HOOK
BARBLESS
LIMERICK
SPROAT LONG SHANK
SPROAT REGULAR
SPROAT FINE WIRE

MODERN HOOKS ARE MADE MOSTLY OF CARBON STEEL... HERE'S THE BREAK-DOWN:

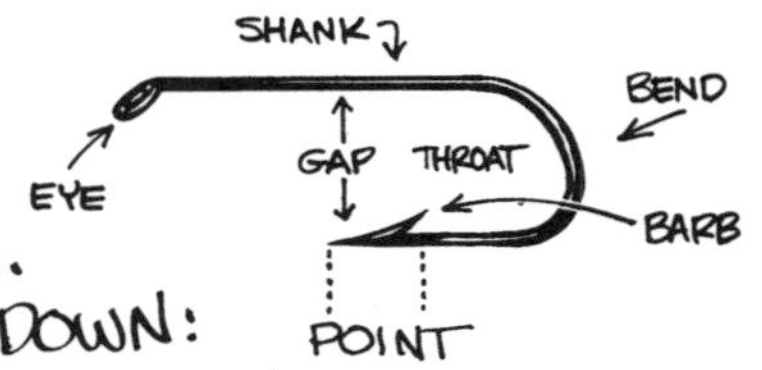

SHANK
EYE
GAP
THROAT
BEND
BARB
POINT

NO. 12 HOOK
NO. 22 HOOK

NAIL KNOT

FOR ATTACHING LINE TO LEADER - USE TINY PLASTIC TUBE SUPPLIED WITH LINE, OR A NAIL... COAT FINISHED KNOT WITH RUBBER BASE GLUE LIKE "PLIOBOND" TO PREVENT SNAGGING ON GUIDES...

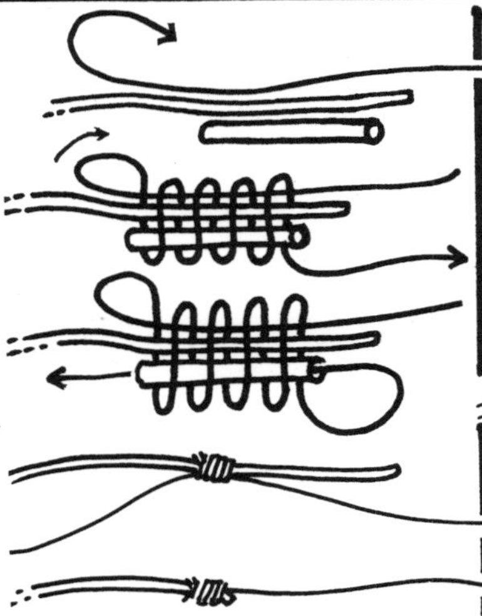

KNOT FOR JOINING LINE TO BACKING

NEEDLE KNOT
-DIFFICULT, BUT SUPERIOR TO NAIL KNOT..

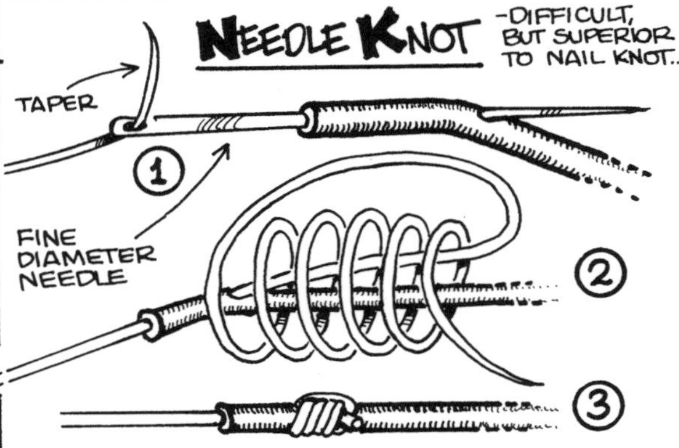

TAPER
FINE DIAMETER NEEDLE
① ② ③

-ANOTHER LINE-TO-LEADER KNOT BUT A #☆◎!! TO DO BECAUSE OF THE NEEDLE BIT...USE PLYERS AND PRAYER..

SURGEON'S KNOT
-FOR JOINING TIPPET TO LEADER....

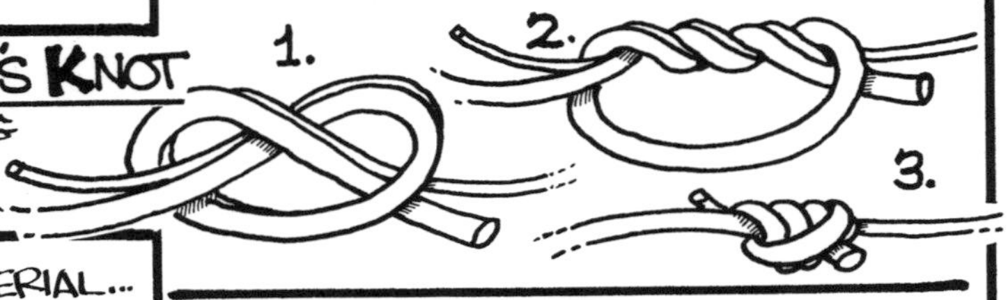

1. 2. 3.

-FOR JOINING LEADER MATERIAL...
BLOOD KNOT
① ② ③
TRIM

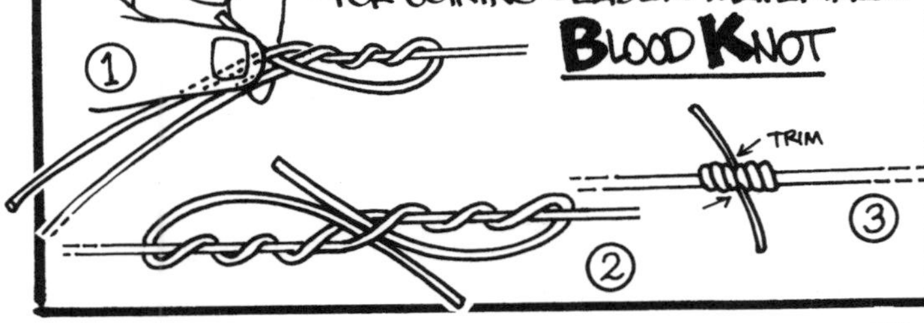

TURLE KNOT - LEADER-TO-FLY..

29

FLY CASTING

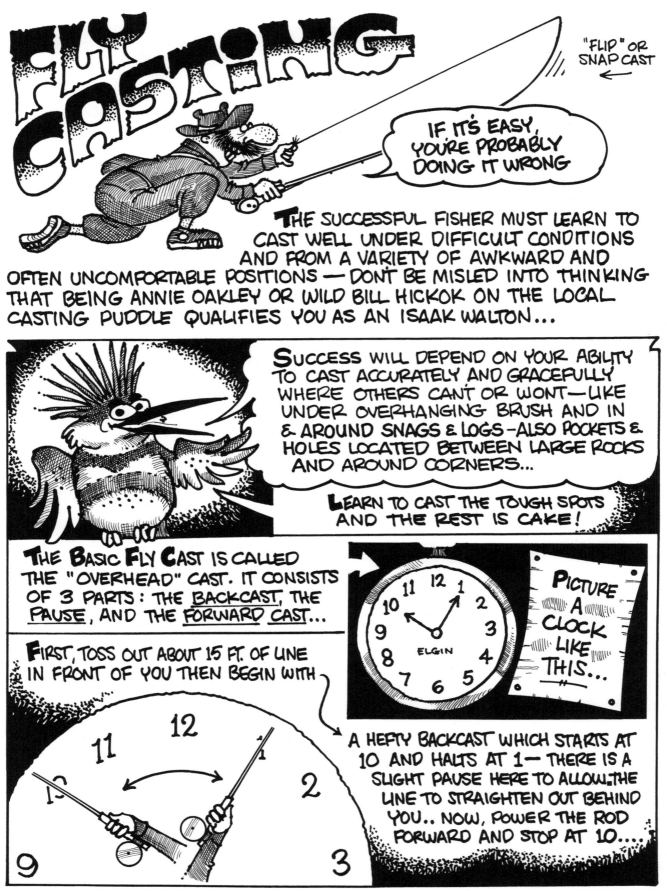

"FLIP" OR SNAP CAST

IF IT'S EASY, YOU'RE PROBABLY DOING IT WRONG

THE SUCCESSFUL FISHER MUST LEARN TO CAST WELL UNDER DIFFICULT CONDITIONS AND FROM A VARIETY OF AWKWARD AND OFTEN UNCOMFORTABLE POSITIONS — DON'T BE MISLED INTO THINKING THAT BEING ANNIE OAKLEY OR WILD BILL HICKOK ON THE LOCAL CASTING PUDDLE QUALIFIES YOU AS AN ISAAK WALTON...

SUCCESS WILL DEPEND ON YOUR ABILITY TO CAST ACCURATELY AND GRACEFULLY WHERE OTHERS CAN'T OR WON'T — LIKE UNDER OVERHANGING BRUSH AND IN & AROUND SNAGS & LOGS — ALSO POCKETS & HOLES LOCATED BETWEEN LARGE ROCKS AND AROUND CORNERS...

LEARN TO CAST THE TOUGH SPOTS AND THE REST IS CAKE!

THE BASIC FLY CAST IS CALLED THE "OVERHEAD" CAST. IT CONSISTS OF 3 PARTS: THE BACKCAST, THE PAUSE, AND THE FORWARD CAST...

FIRST, TOSS OUT ABOUT 15 FT. OF LINE IN FRONT OF YOU THEN BEGIN WITH

PICTURE A CLOCK LIKE THIS...

ELGIN

A HEFTY BACKCAST WHICH STARTS AT 10 AND HALTS AT 1 — THERE IS A SLIGHT PAUSE HERE TO ALLOW THE LINE TO STRAIGHTEN OUT BEHIND YOU.. NOW, POWER THE ROD FORWARD AND STOP AT 10....

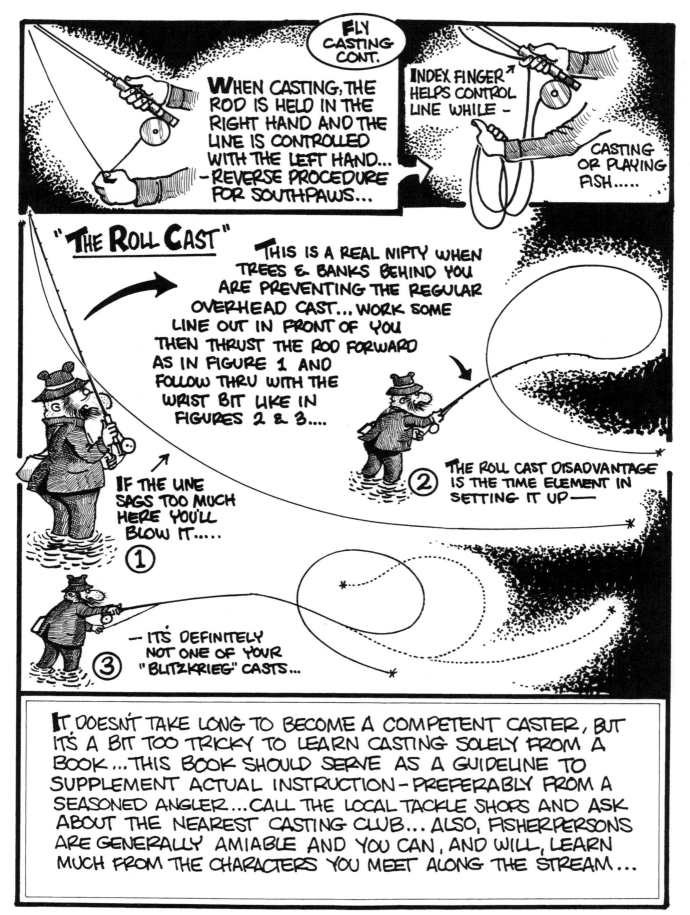

THE HORIZONTAL or SIDE CAST

JUST THE TICKET FOR DEALING WITH OVERHANGING TREES AND BRUSH. THE MECHANICS ARE THE SAME AS THE OVERHEAD CAST....

–ALSO USED WHEN STALKING AT CLOSE RANGE IN ORDER TO PREVENT TROUT FROM SPOOKING AT THE SHADOW OR SILHOUETTE OF YOUR ROD TIP....

THE STEEPLE or TOWER CAST

ANOTHER VARIANT OF THE OVERHEAD CAST. THE HIGH BACK-CAST IS UTILIZED TO AVOID TREES AND OTHER LARGE OBJECTS....

② ①

THE FALSE CAST

Bogus!

THIS IS A PREPARATORY MOVEMENT THAT, QUITE SIMPLY, CONSISTS OF CASTING YOUR FLY BACK AND FORTH WITHOUT LETTING IT TOUCH THE WATER. ITS PURPOSES ARE TO DRY OUT THE FLY SO THAT IT FLOATS BETTER AND TO AID IN LINING UP THE TARGET..,–THREE FALSE CASTS ARE USUALLY SUFFICIENT...

DAPPING — "FLYCASTING'S STEPCHILD"

DAPPING IS THE UNCELEBRATED BUT WORTHY ART OF EASING YOUR ROD TIP THRU THE BUSHES AND SETTING THE FLY ON THE WATER. IT'S AN EXTREMELY EFFECTIVE TECHNIQUE AND WILL USUALLY PRODUCE WHEN ALL ELSE FAILS...

LIKE A STATUE

STRIKING MIGHT BE IMPOSSIBLE, BUT THE FISH WILL PROBABLY HOOK ITSELF BECAUSE OF THE TAUT LINE.

DON'T GO CHARGING INTO THE BRUSH LIKE A CAPE BUFFALO; YOUR VIBRATIONS WILL BE TRANSMITTED TO THE FISH VIA THE ROOTS...

DAPPING WITH LIVE BAIT IS THE SAME THING EXCEPT THAT THE ENTICEMENT IS OFTEN SUBMERGED A FEW INCHES, POSSIBLY WITH THE AID OF A SPLIT SHOT OR TWIST-ON SINKER...

"THE CURTIS CREEK SNEAK"

THE FLY IS HELD UNTIL READY TO CAST...

—ROD KEPT LOW AND TO THE REAR WHILE APPROACHING...

IF YOU THINK ALL THIS CREEPING & CRAWLING A BIT LUDICROUS—

—YOU'LL GET OVER IT

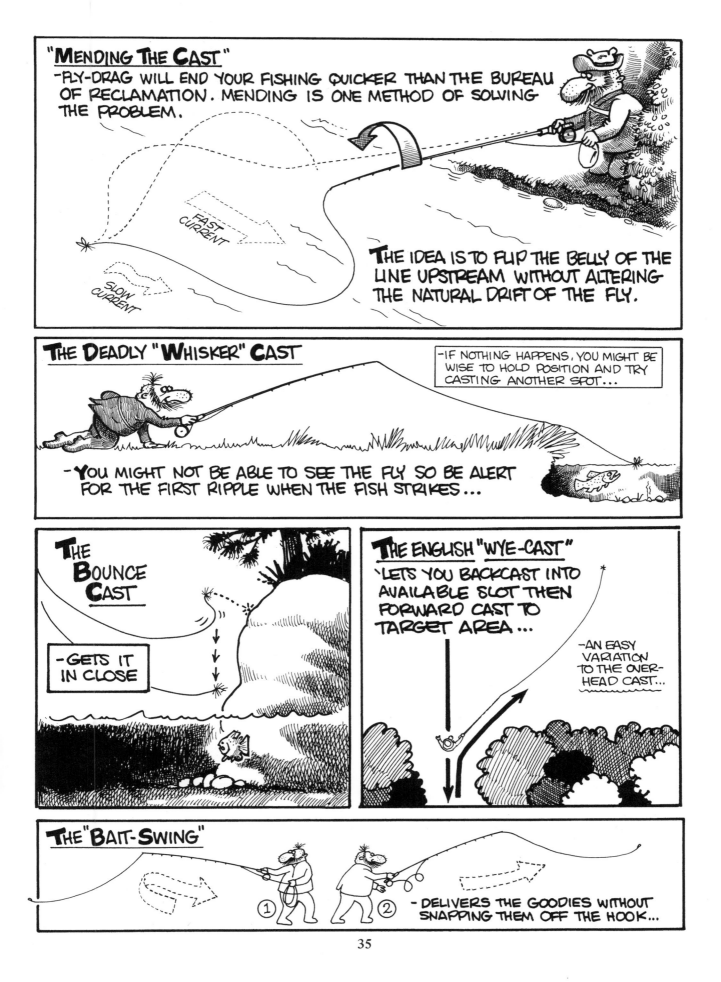

"MENDING THE CAST"

—FLY-DRAG WILL END YOUR FISHING QUICKER THAN THE BUREAU OF RECLAMATION. MENDING IS ONE METHOD OF SOLVING THE PROBLEM.

FAST CURRENT

SLOW CURRENT

THE IDEA IS TO FLIP THE BELLY OF THE LINE UPSTREAM WITHOUT ALTERING THE NATURAL DRIFT OF THE FLY.

THE DEADLY "WHISKER" CAST

—IF NOTHING HAPPENS, YOU MIGHT BE WISE TO HOLD POSITION AND TRY CASTING ANOTHER SPOT...

—YOU MIGHT NOT BE ABLE TO SEE THE FLY SO BE ALERT FOR THE FIRST RIPPLE WHEN THE FISH STRIKES...

THE BOUNCE CAST

—GETS IT IN CLOSE

THE ENGLISH "WYE-CAST"

—LETS YOU BACKCAST INTO AVAILABLE SLOT THEN FORWARD CAST TO TARGET AREA...

—AN EASY VARIATION TO THE OVER-HEAD CAST...

THE "BAIT-SWING"

① ②

—DELIVERS THE GOODIES WITHOUT SNAPPING THEM OFF THE HOOK...

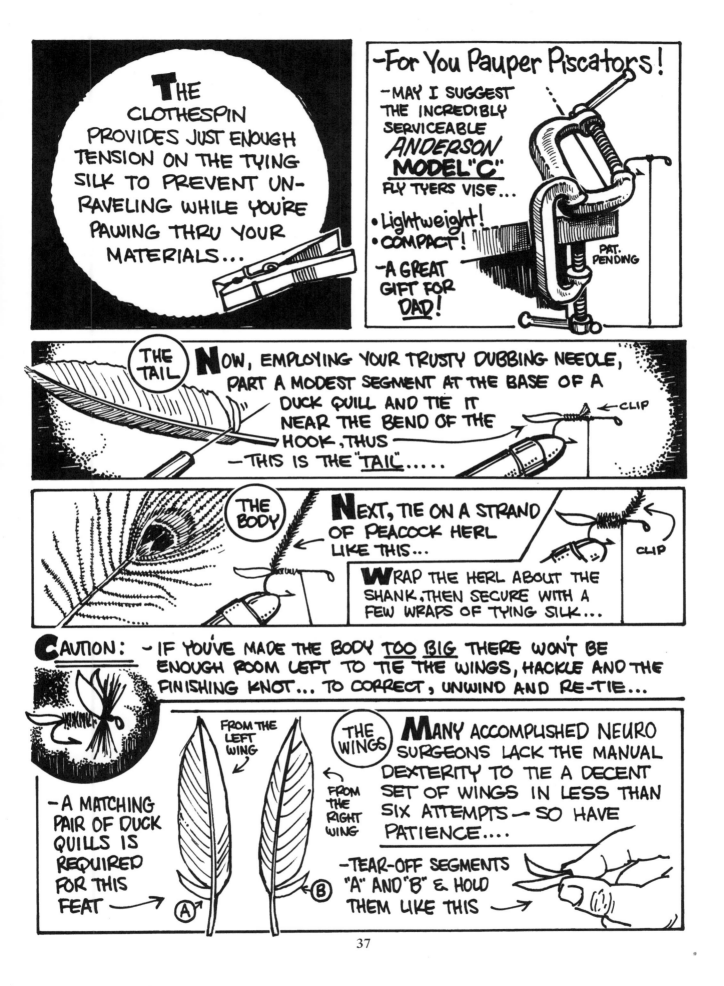

THE CLOTHESPIN PROVIDES JUST ENOUGH TENSION ON THE TYING SILK TO PREVENT UN-RAVELING WHILE YOU'RE PAWING THRU YOUR MATERIALS...

-For You Pauper Piscators!

-MAY I SUGGEST THE INCREDIBLY SERVICEABLE *ANDERSON MODEL "C"* FLY TYERS VISE...

• Lightweight!
• COMPACT!

-A GREAT GIFT FOR *DAD!*

PAT. PENDING

THE TAIL

NOW, EMPLOYING YOUR TRUSTY DUBBING NEEDLE, PART A MODEST SEGMENT AT THE BASE OF A DUCK QUILL AND TIE IT NEAR THE BEND OF THE HOOK, THUS -THIS IS THE "TAIL".....

←CLIP

THE BODY

NEXT, TIE ON A STRAND OF PEACOCK HERL LIKE THIS...

WRAP THE HERL ABOUT THE SHANK, THEN SECURE WITH A FEW WRAPS OF TYING SILK...

CLIP

CAUTION: -IF YOU'VE MADE THE BODY *TOO BIG* THERE WON'T BE ENOUGH ROOM LEFT TO TIE THE WINGS, HACKLE AND THE FINISHING KNOT... TO CORRECT, UNWIND AND RE-TIE...

THE WINGS

FROM THE LEFT WING

FROM THE RIGHT WING

MANY ACCOMPLISHED NEURO SURGEONS LACK THE MANUAL DEXTERITY TO TIE A DECENT SET OF WINGS IN LESS THAN SIX ATTEMPTS — SO HAVE PATIENCE....

-A MATCHING PAIR OF DUCK QUILLS IS REQUIRED FOR THIS FEAT →

Ⓐ

Ⓑ

-TEAR-OFF SEGMENTS "A" AND "B" & HOLD THEM LIKE THIS →

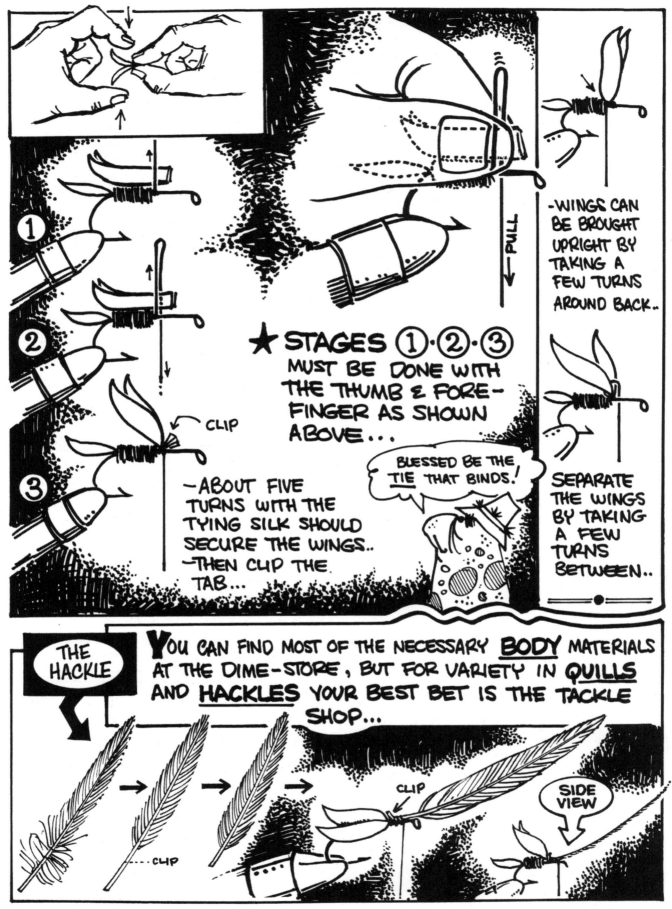

① ② ③

★ STAGES ①·②·③ MUST BE DONE WITH THE THUMB & FORE-FINGER AS SHOWN ABOVE...

CLIP

—ABOUT FIVE TURNS WITH THE TYING SILK SHOULD SECURE THE WINGS.. —THEN CLIP THE TAB...

BLESSED BE THE TIE THAT BINDS!

PULL

—WINGS CAN BE BROUGHT UPRIGHT BY TAKING A FEW TURNS AROUND BACK..

SEPARATE THE WINGS BY TAKING A FEW TURNS BETWEEN..

THE HACKLE

YOU CAN FIND MOST OF THE NECESSARY **BODY** MATERIALS AT THE DIME-STORE, BUT FOR VARIETY IN **QUILLS** AND **HACKLES** YOUR BEST BET IS THE TACKLE SHOP...

...CLIP

CLIP

SIDE VIEW

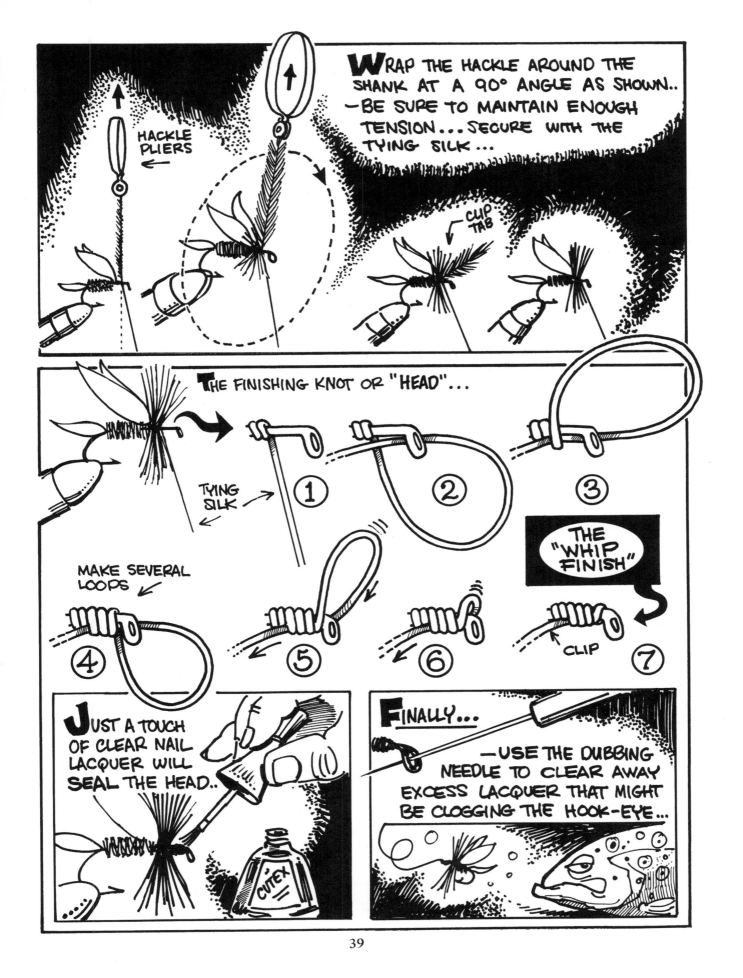

WRAP THE HACKLE AROUND THE SHANK AT A 90° ANGLE AS SHOWN.. —BE SURE TO MAINTAIN ENOUGH TENSION...SECURE WITH THE TYING SILK...

HACKLE PLIERS

CLIP TAB

THE FINISHING KNOT OR "HEAD"...

TYING SILK

① ② ③

MAKE SEVERAL LOOPS

④ ⑤ ⑥

THE "WHIP FINISH"

CLIP ⑦

JUST A TOUCH OF CLEAR NAIL LACQUER WILL SEAL THE HEAD..

CUTEX

FINALLY... —USE THE DUBBING NEEDLE TO CLEAR AWAY EXCESS LACQUER THAT MIGHT BE CLOGGING THE HOOK-EYE...

BACKPACKING for TROUT

BACKPACKING IS THE ART OF KNOWING WHAT NOT TO TAKE.. KEEP YOUR FISHING KIT LIGHT AND SIMPLE..-THIS USUALLY MEANS ELIMINATING WADERS, HIP BOOTS, LANDING NET AND FLY TYING KIT... IF YOU FEEL THAT WADING IS NECESSARY, TAKE A PAIR OF CANVAS SNEAKERS... (OR GYM SHOES)

-THE ROD CASE CAN BE TIED TO THE OUTSIDE OF THE PACK...

-AN EXTRA LONG ROD CASE CAN BE CARRIED AND EMPLOYED AS A WALKING STICK IF IT IS STOUT ENOUGH...

-THE CREEL CAN BE HUNG ON THE PACK...

-THE ASSEMBLED ROD .. AND REEL CAN BE CARRIED IN-HAND FOR FISHING EN-ROUTE...

FIGURE ON A MINIMUM OF 4 FLIES FOR EACH DAY YOU ACTUALLY FISH..

CLEAN EACH FISH AS YOU CATCH IT.
-WRAP IN DRY GRASS AND PLACE IN CREEL.

DRYING THE FISH AFTER CLEANING HELPS SLOW-DOWN THE BACTERIAL ACTION...

TROUT WILL USUALLY KEEP OVERNIGHT PROVIDED THEY HAVE BEEN CLEANED AND KEPT COOL AND DRY FROM THE MOMENT THEY'RE CAUGHT.
HANG THEM IN THE SHADE WHEN YOU RETURN TO CAMP.

DRY EACH TROUT SEPARATELY

IF YOU DESIRE A GOOD 8½' ROD THAT FITS INTO A 24" CASE FOR BACK-PACKING...

24" —I CAN RECOMMEND THE "FENWICK" #FF856-5
-THE LINE SPECIFICATION SAYS 6 BUT I PREFER A 5.

6' 6'
⅛" CORD
12 FEET

METHOD FOR HANGING FISH AND CREEL IN BEAR COUNTRY..

A DOWN VEST IS A WORTHY ITEM.. CUTS THE CHILL WHILE ALLOWING THE ARMS FREE FOR CASTING. STUFFS INTO A SMALL BAG FOR BACKPACKING. WEIGHS ALMOST NOTHING.

—"OLD EPHRAIM"
-TO AVOID AN UN-NECESSARY CON-FRONTATION, KEEP FISH AND FOOD SMELLS AWAY FROM YOUR PACK, YOUR CAMP, AND YOUR TENT...

-EXCEPT WHEN COOKING & EATING

AN INVESTMENT IN A MOUNTAIN TENT MEANS A COZY SHELTER WHEN THE STORM RAGES. GREAT FOR CAR CAMPING TOO.
SHOULD INCLUDE A RAIN FLY..

-CARRY A SMALL C-CLAMP, A FEW EXTRA HOOKS AND A SPOOL OF THREAD AS AN EMERGENCY FLY-TYING KIT.. YOU CAN FASHION EFFECTIVE FLIES OUT OF ALMOST ANY THING AROUND CAMP - EVEN HUMAN HAIR. I USUALLY TRY TO BRING ALONG A BLONDE FOR LIGHTER PATTERNS.

A BACKPACKER STOVE IS A MUST FOR COOKING WHERE WOOD IS SCARCE.

"GUDDLING"-"TICKLING" CATCHING TROUT WITH YOUR BARE HANDS...

1. DELIBERATELY SCARE THE FISH AND KEEP TRACK OF THEM AS THEY SCURRY TO HIDE UNDER THE BANKS OR BENEATH BRANCHES AND FLOATING DEBRIS..

2. COOL YOUR HANDS...

3. UTILIZING A STICK, A HAND OR A FRIEND STIR UP SOME MUCK ABOVE WHERE YOUR QUARRY IS HIDING — THE MUCK WILL DRIFT BACK INTO THE SANCTUARY AND MASK THE FORTHCOMING TREACHERY..

4. THIS MANEUVER WILL BE HIGHLY FACILITATED IF YOU HAPPEN TO BE AN ORANG-OUTANG — MOVE YOUR HANDS SLOWLY TOWARD THE FISH. IF POSSIBLE TRY TO GET ONE HAND UNDER THE FISH NEAR ITS HEAD — THE OTHER JUST ABOVE THE TAIL. EASY NOW...

IF THE TROUT DARTS QUICKLY AWAY RATHER THAN JUST MOVING SLOWLY FROM ITS POSITION, YOU'VE MADE AN ERROR. ONLY YOUR REPEATED EFFORTS WILL TELL YOU WHERE YOU'VE GONE WRONG. IF APPROACHED PROPERLY THE CREATURE WILL SELDOM DO MORE THAN TRY TO WIGGLE AND BURROW FURTHER INTO ITS SANCTUARY...

5. SO ONCE YOU'VE GOT YOUR HANDS ABOUT THE EVASIVE BEAST, SLOWLY AND GENTLY BUT FIRMLY CLOSE THEM ...

← CURRENT

TOP VIEW

ROD MEDICINE

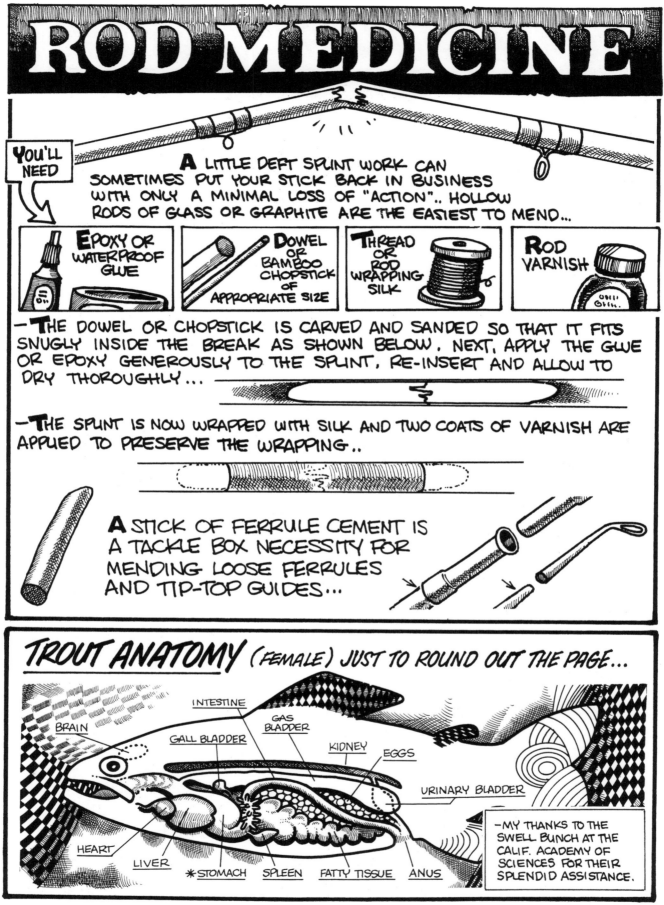

You'll Need

A LITTLE DEFT SPLINT WORK CAN SOMETIMES PUT YOUR STICK BACK IN BUSINESS WITH ONLY A MINIMAL LOSS OF "ACTION".. HOLLOW RODS OF GLASS OR GRAPHITE ARE THE EASIEST TO MEND...

- **E**POXY OR WATERPROOF GLUE
- **D**OWEL OR BAMBOO CHOPSTICK OF APPROPRIATE SIZE
- **T**HREAD OR ROD WRAPPING SILK
- **R**OD VARNISH

—**T**HE DOWEL OR CHOPSTICK IS CARVED AND SANDED SO THAT IT FITS SNUGLY INSIDE THE BREAK AS SHOWN BELOW. NEXT, APPLY THE GLUE OR EPOXY GENEROUSLY TO THE SPLINT, RE-INSERT AND ALLOW TO DRY THOROUGHLY...

—**T**HE SPLINT IS NOW WRAPPED WITH SILK AND TWO COATS OF VARNISH ARE APPLIED TO PRESERVE THE WRAPPING..

A STICK OF FERRULE CEMENT IS A TACKLE BOX NECESSITY FOR MENDING LOOSE FERRULES AND TIP-TOP GUIDES...

TROUT ANATOMY (FEMALE) JUST TO ROUND OUT THE PAGE...

BRAIN
INTESTINE
GALL BLADDER
GAS BLADDER
KIDNEY
EGGS
URINARY BLADDER
HEART
LIVER
*STOMACH
SPLEEN
FATTY TISSUE
ANUS

—MY THANKS TO THE SWELL BUNCH AT THE CALIF. ACADEMY OF SCIENCES FOR THEIR SPLENDID ASSISTANCE.

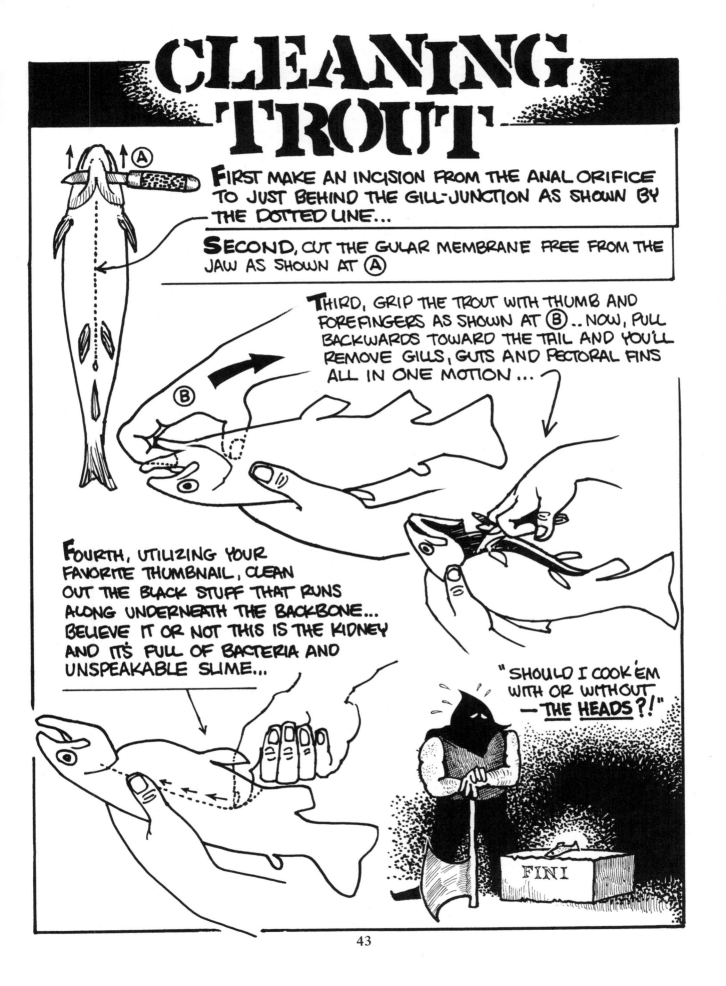

TROUT COOKING

YOU'LL NEED

A MATCH

SALT

GRASS (LEGAL)

FIREWOOD

CLEANED TROUT

FRESH WATER

① MAKE A FIRE AND LET BURN UNTIL IT BUILDS UP A SUBSTANTIAL PILE OF GLOWING EMBERS....

② SALT THE INSIDES OF EACH TROUT —DON'T BE STINGY...

③ SOAK THE GRASS IN WATER AND WRAP TROUT...

④ BURY THE WRAPPED TROUT IN THE EMBERS LIKE THIS.. — COOKING TIME VARIES SOMEWHAT DEPENDING ON THE SIZE OF THE FISH BUT WHEN THE GRASS STARTS BURNING YOU CAN ALMOST BET THAT THE MORSEL IS NEARING PERFECTION...

THERE ARE DOZENS OF WAYS TO COOK TROUT —TRY DIPPING THEM IN A SEASONED EGG-BATTER AND FRYING IN BUTTER....

GIANT TROUT CAN BE STUFFED AND BAKED WITH AN APPLE IN IT'S MOUTH....

TIPS & CONTRIVANCES

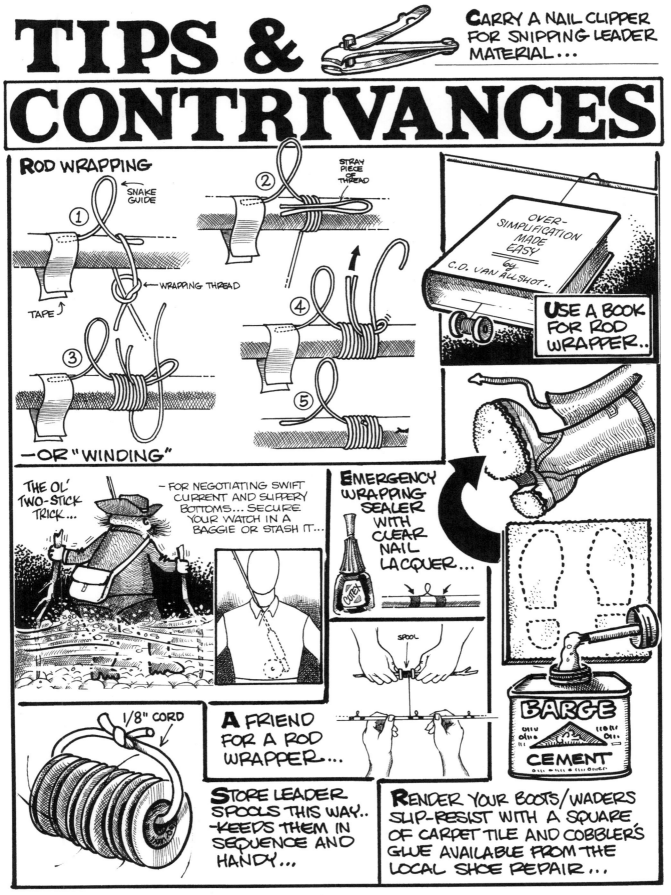

CARRY A NAIL CLIPPER FOR SNIPPING LEADER MATERIAL...

ROD WRAPPING

① SNAKE GUIDE

WRAPPING THREAD

TAPE

② STRAY PIECE OF THREAD

③

④

⑤

—OR "WINDING"

OVER-SIMPLIFICATION MADE EASY by C.O. VAN ALLSHOT..

USE A BOOK FOR ROD WRAPPER..

THE OL' TWO-STICK TRICK...

— FOR NEGOTIATING SWIFT CURRENT AND SLIPPERY BOTTOMS... SECURE YOUR WATCH IN A BAGGIE OR STASH IT...

EMERGENCY WRAPPING SEALER WITH CLEAR NAIL LACQUER...

Cutex

SPOOL

1/8" CORD

A FRIEND FOR A ROD WRAPPER....

STORE LEADER SPOOLS THIS WAY.. -KEEPS THEM IN SEQUENCE AND HANDY...

BARGE CEMENT

RENDER YOUR BOOTS/WADERS SLIP-RESIST WITH A SQUARE OF CARPET TILE AND COBBLER'S GLUE AVAILABLE FROM THE LOCAL SHOE REPAIR...

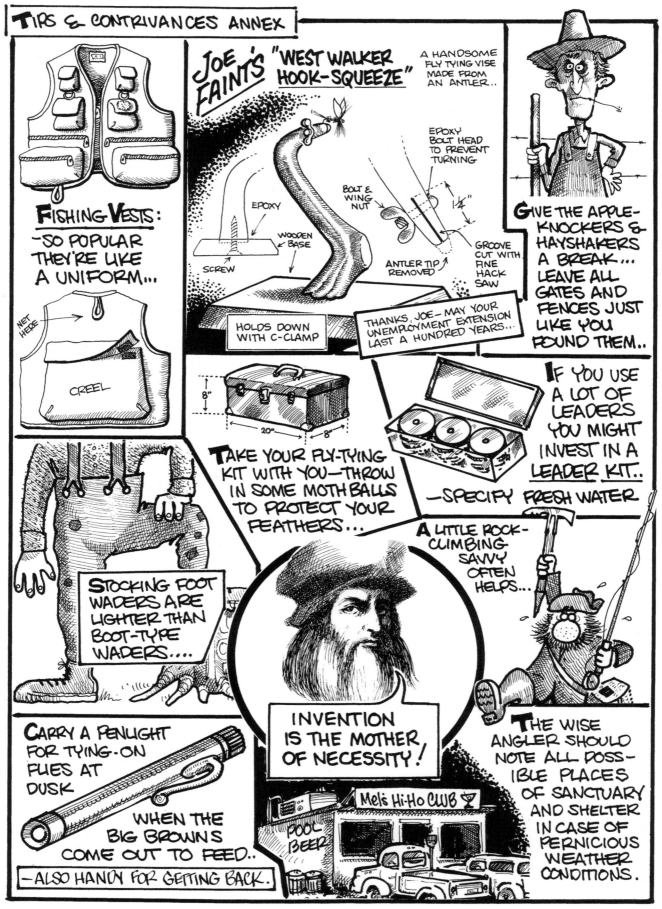

FISHING VESTS:
—SO POPULAR THEY'RE LIKE A UNIFORM...

NET HERE

CREEL

JOE FAINT'S "WEST WALKER HOOK-SQUEEZE"

A HANDSOME FLY TYING VISE MADE FROM AN ANTLER..

EPOXY

WOODEN BASE

SCREW

EPOXY BOLT HEAD TO PREVENT TURNING

BOLT & WING NUT

1¼"

ANTLER TIP REMOVED

GROOVE CUT WITH FINE HACK SAW

HOLDS DOWN WITH C-CLAMP

THANKS, JOE— MAY YOUR UNEMPLOYMENT EXTENSION LAST A HUNDRED YEARS...

GIVE THE APPLE-KNOCKERS & HAYSHAKERS A BREAK... LEAVE ALL GATES AND FENCES JUST LIKE YOU FOUND THEM..

IF YOU USE A LOT OF LEADERS YOU MIGHT INVEST IN A LEADER KIT..
—SPECIFY FRESH WATER

8"
20"
8"

TAKE YOUR FLY-TYING KIT WITH YOU—THROW IN SOME MOTH BALLS TO PROTECT YOUR FEATHERS...

STOCKING FOOT WADERS ARE LIGHTER THAN BOOT-TYPE WADERS....

A LITTLE ROCK-CLIMBING SAVVY OFTEN HELPS...

INVENTION IS THE MOTHER OF NECESSITY!

THE WISE ANGLER SHOULD NOTE ALL POSS-IBLE PLACES OF SANCTUARY AND SHELTER IN CASE OF PERNICIOUS WEATHER CONDITIONS.

CARRY A PENLIGHT FOR TYING-ON FLIES AT DUSK

WHEN THE BIG BROWNS COME OUT TO FEED..

—ALSO HANDY FOR GETTING BACK.

Mel's Hi-Ho CLUB
POOL
BEER

THE PRIORITIES OF THE GAME

HERE ARE THE FIVE MOST ESSENTIAL DISCIPLINES IN BECOMING A GOOD FLY FISHERPERSON:

CASTING: YOU'VE FULFILLED THIS REQUIREMENT IF YOU CAN PERFORM A TOLERABLY VIRTUOUS OVERHEAD CAST, SIDE CAST, STEEPLE CAST, WYE CAST AND CURTIS CREEK SNEAK CAST...

SELECTING THE FLY: THE FLY SHOULD APPROXIMATE THE SIZE, SHAPE AND COLOR OF WHATEVER THE FISH MIGHT BE TAKING — FIND OUT BY GATHERING YOUR OWN SAMPLES; INQUIRING AT THE LOCAL TACKLE SHOP AND ASKING OTHER FISHERMEN...

STALKING: STALKING IS THE KEY TO BECOMING A GOOD FLY FISHER. WITHOUT STALKING YOU WON'T GET ANY ACTION (STRIKES) AND UNLESS YOU GET LOTS OF ACTION YOU CAN'T BECOME PROFICIENT AT RECOGNIZING STRIKES OR BEING ABLE TO READ THE WATER...WHEN I WAS A KID I USED TO PRETEND THAT EACH LIKELY-LOOKING SPOT WAS AN ENEMY MACHINE GUN NEST AND WOULD APPROACH IT ACCORDINGLY — ONE FALSE MOVE AND IT WUZ CURTAINS FOR ME AND THE WHOLE PLATOON...

RECOGNIZING THE STRIKE: THE MORE STRIKES YOU GET THE BETTER AND FASTER YOU GET AT RECOGNIZING THEM. THAT'S THE WAY IT GOES...

READING THE WATER: YOU LEARN WHERE THE FISH ARE BY ACTUALLY SEEING THEM. HERE ARE THE WAYS:
- A. BY OBSERVING THEM AS YOU FISH OR WALK ALONG.
- B. BY SEEING THEM BREAK THE SURFACE WHEN THEY FEED.
- C. BY SEEING THEM WHEN THEY HIT YOUR FLY (STRIKE.)

ANGLING EXPERTISE IS A HIGHLY COORDINATED SYNTHESIS OF SKILLFUL CASTING, IMAGINATIVE STALKING, KEEN VISION, QUICK REFLEXES, PLENTY OF SAVVY AND LOTS OF EXPERIENCE...

47

SANITY, ANYONE?

MOST OF THE WATERS I FISHED AS A KID HAVE BEEN CHANNELED, PIPED OR DAMMED. GREEDY LITTLE MINDS ARE EVER BUSY CONVERTING OUR LANDSCAPES INTO SLAG-HEAPS, HOUSING TRACTS, CANALS, FREEWAYS AND SHOPPING MALLS, A PERVERSION THEY ZEALOUSLY PURSUE UNDER THE RAGGED BANNER OF PROGRESS.

ON THIS DOUR BUT PROPHETIC NOTE I HEREBY SUBMIT THE NAMES OF TWO ORGANIZATIONS THAT SPEAK ON BEHALF OF OUR RIVERS, LAKES AND STREAMS:

FEDERATION OF FLY FISHERMEN
519 MAIN ST., EL SEGUNDO, CA. 90245

•

TROUT UNLIMITED...
P.O. BOX 361 DENVER, COLO. 80201

IS THERE REALLY A CURTIS CREEK?

POSSIBLY, MY DARLINGS, QUITE POSSIBLY; BUT I WILL SAY NO MORE BECAUSE THAT IS YOUR FINAL LESSON: TO GO FORTH AND SEEK YOUR OWN CURTIS CREEK ~ A DELIGHTFUL, UNSPOILED STRETCH OF WATER THAT YOU WILL CHERISH ABOVE ALL OTHERS... THERE ARE FEW CURTIS CREEKS IN THIS LIFE SO WHEN YOU FIND IT, KEEP ITS SECRET WELL...

My thanks to the bright lads at Creative Sports and S.F. Fly Fisherman for their help in this revision...